GROWINGDEEPER

WHOLE PRAYER

Speaking and Listening to God

WALTER WANGERIN JR.
Foreword by Eugene Peterson

ZondervanPublishingHouse
Grand Rapids, Michigan

A Division of HarperCollins*Publishers*

Whole Prayer
Copyright © 1998 by Walter Wangerin Jr.

Requests for information should be addressed to:

ZondervanPublishingHouse
Grand Rapids, Michigan 49530

Library of Congress Cataloging-in-Publication Data

Wangerin, Walter.
    Whole prayer : speaking and listening to God / Walter Wangerin.
       p. cm.
    ISBN: 0-310-20197-7
    1. Prayer—Christianity.   I. Title.
BV215.W36   1997
248.3'2—DC21
                                                             97–21635
                                                                     CIP

This edition printed on acid-free paper and meets the American National
Standards Institute Z39.48 standard.

All Scripture quotations, unless otherwise indicated, are taken from the King
James Version, the Revised Standard Version, or are the author's own original
translation.

Published in association with the literary agency of Alive Communications, Inc.,
1465 Kelly Johnson Blvd., Suite 320, Colorado Springs, CO 80920.

Interior design by Sue Koppenol

Printed in the United States of America

98 99 00 01 02 03 04 / ❖ DC/ 10 9 8 7 6 5 4 3

*To the group of friends with whom I prayed
in laughter and in anguish,
for so many years
in Evansville,
this book is dedicated:*

*Rita Cooksey
Mark Kroeger
Cheryl Lawrence
Phil Lawrence
Brenda Piper
Butch Piper
Thanne Wangerin*

CONTENTS

FOREWORD
BY EUGENE H. PETERSON

A favorite story in our home as our children were growing up was of John Muir at the top of the Douglas fir in the storm.* Whenever we were assaulted by thunder and lightning, rain sluicing out of the sky, and the five of us, parents and three children, huddled together on the porch enjoying the dangerous fireworks from our safe ringside seat, one of the kids would say, "Tell us the John Muir story, Daddy!" And I'd tell it again.

In the last half of the nineteenth century, John Muir was our most intrepid and worshipful explorer of the western extremities of our North American continent. For decades he tramped up and down through our God-created wonders, from the California Sierras to the Alaskan glaciers, observing, reporting, praising, and experiencing—entering into whatever he found with childlike delight and mature reverence.

At one period during this time (the year was 1874) Muir visited a friend who had a cabin, snug in a valley of one of the tributaries of the Yuba River in the Sierra Mountains—a place from which to venture into the wilderness and then return for a comforting cup of tea.

One December day a storm moved in from the Pacific—a fierce storm that bent the junipers and pines, the madronas and fir trees as if they were so many blades of

---

*Edwin Way Teale, ed. *The Wilderness World of John Muir* (Boston: Houghton Mifflin, 1954), 181–90.

grass. It was for just such times this cabin had been built: cozy protection from the harsh elements. We easily imagine Muir and his host safe and secure in his tightly caulked cabin, a fire blazing against the cruel assault of the elements, wrapped in sheepskins, Muir meditatively rendering the wildness into his elegant prose. But our imaginations, not trained to cope with Muir, betray us. For Muir, instead of retreating to the coziness of the cabin, pulling the door tight, and throwing another stick of wood on the fire, strode *out* of the cabin into the storm, climbed a high ridge, picked a giant Douglas fir as the best perch for experiencing the kaleidoscope of color and sound, scent and motion, scrambled his way to the top, and rode out the storm, lashed by the wind, holding on for dear life, relishing *Weather*, taking it all in—its rich sensuality, its primal energy.

Throughout its many retellings, the story of John Muir, storm-whipped at the top of the Douglas fir in the Yuba River valley, gradually took shape as a kind of icon of Christian spirituality for our family. The icon has been in place ever since as a standing rebuke against becoming a mere spectator to life, preferring creature comforts to Creator confrontations.

For spirituality has to do with life, *lived* life. For Christians, "spirituality" is derived (always and exclusively) from Spirit, God's Holy Spirit. And "spirit," in the biblical languages of Hebrew and Greek, is the word "wind," or "breeze," or "breath"—an invisibility that has visible effects.

This is the Wind/Spirit that created all the life we both see and can't see (Genesis 1:2); that created the life

10

of Jesus (Luke 1:35 and 3:22); that created a church of worshiping men and women (Acts 2:2–4); that creates each Christian (Romans 8:11). There is no accounting for life, any life, except by means of this Wind/Spirit:

> *Thou sendest forth thy spirit [breath/wind], they are created:*
> *and thou renewest the face of the earth. (Psalm 104:30 KJV)*

There is clearly far more to Spirit-created living than can be detected by blood pressure and pulse rate. All the "vital signs" of botany, biology, and physiology combined hardly begin to account for life; if it doesn't also extend into matters far more complex than our circulatory and respiratory systems—namely, matters of joy and love, faith and hope, truth and beauty, meaning and value—there is simply not enough there to qualify as "life" for the common run of human beings on this planet earth. Most of us may not be able to define "spirituality" in a satisfactory way, but few of us fail to recognize its presence or absence. And to feel ourselves enhanced by its presence and diminished by its absence. Life, life, and more life— it's our deepest hunger and thirst.

But that doesn't always translate into Spirit, Spirit, and more Spirit in the conduct of our lives. Spirit, *Holy* Spirit, in Christian terminology, is God's life in our lives, God living in us and thereby making us participants in the extravagant prodigality of life, visible and invisible, that is Spirit-created.

We humans, somewhere along the way, seem to have picked up the bad habit of trying to get life on our terms, without all the bother of God, the Spirit of Life. We keep trying to be our own gods; and we keep making a sorry mess of it. Worse, the word has gotten around in recent years that "spirituality" itself might be a way of getting a more intense life without having to deal with God—spirituality as a kind of intuitive bypass around the inconvenience of repentance and sacrifice and putting ourselves at risk by following Jesus in the way of the cross, the very way Jesus plainly told was the only way to the "abundant life" that he had come to bless us with.

The generic name for this way of going about things—trying to put together a life of meaning and security out of God-sanctioned stories and routines, salted with weekends of diversion and occasional erotic interludes, without dealing firsthand, believingly and obediently, with God—is "religion." It is not, of course, a life without God, but the God who is there tends to be mostly background and resource—a Quality or Being that provides the ideas and energy that I take charge of and arrange and use as I see fit. We all of us do it, more or less.

The word "religion," following one possible etymology (not all agree on this), comes from the Latin, *religere*, "to bind up, or tie up, again." The picture that comes to my mind is of myself, having spent years "getting it all together," strolling through John Muir's Yuba River valley, enjoying the country, whistling in self-satisfaction, carrying my "life" bundled in a neat package—memories and morals, goals and diversions, prayers and devotion all sorted and tied together. And then the storm comes, fierce and sudden, a gust tears my packaged life from my arms and scatters the items every which way, all over the valley, all through the forest.

What do I then do? Do I run helter-skelter through the trees, crawl through the brush, frantically trying to recover all the pieces of my life, desperately enlisting the help of passersby and calling in the experts, searching for and retrieving and putting back together again (rebinding!) whatever I can salvage of my life, and then hiding out in the warm and secure cabin until the storm blows over? Or do I follow John Muir to the exposed ridge and the top of the Douglas fir, and open myself to the Weather, not wanting to miss a detail of this invasion of Life into my life, ready at the drop of a hat to lose my life to save it (Mark 8:35)?

For me, the life of religion (cautious and anxious, holding things together as best I can so that my life will make sense and, hopefully, please God), and the life of spirituality (a passion for life and a willingness to risk identity and security in following Jesus, no matter what) contrast in these two scenarios. There is no question regarding what I want: I want to be out in the Weather! But far more often than not I find myself crawling around on the ground, gathering up the pieces of my life and tying them together again in a secure bundle, safe from the effects of the Weather. Actually, the two ways of life can coexist; there is, after all, a place for steady and responsible routine—John Muir, after all, didn't spend all his time at the top of the Douglas fir; he spent most of his time on the valley floor. He also had a cabin that he had built with his own hands in which he received guests and prepared meals for them. But if there is no readiness to respond to the living God, who moves when and how and where he chooses, it isn't much of a life—the *livingness* soon leaks out of it.

∾

We cannot, of course, command Weather. It is there; it happens. There is no question of managing or directing it. There is no recipe for concocting "spirituality" any

more than there is a chemical formula for creating "life."
As Jesus most famously put it to that expert on the religious life, Nicodemus, "You know well enough how the wind blows this way and that. You hear it rustling through the trees, but you have no idea where it comes from or where it's headed next. That's the way it is with everyone 'born from above' by the wind of God, the Spirit of God" (John 3:8 THE MESSAGE).

The best we can do is to cultivate awareness, alertness, so that when the Wind blows we are *there*, ready to step into it—or not: when the absurd command comes to distribute the meager five loaves and two fish to the crowd we are ready to obey—or not; when direction is given to wait with the 120 for the promise, we are ready to wait—or not; when the invitation comes to "take . . . eat . . . drink," we are ready to come to the supper—or not.

⌒〰〰〰〰⌒

The books in this series, *Growing Deeper*, are what some of my friends and I do to stay alert and aware as we wait for the Wind to blow whether in furious storm or cooling breeze or gentle breathing—intending to cultivate and maintain a receptive readiness to the Spirit who brings us Life. They are not books *about* spirituality; they are simply accounts of what we do to stay awake to the Coming. There is nothing novel in any of them; our intent is to report what Christians have commonly done to stay present to the Spirit: we pray (Wangerin), preach and teach (Miller), meditate on the soul (Shaw), reflect on our checkered experiences with God's people (Yancey), and nurture Jesus-friends (Peterson).

Our shared conviction is that most of us in this "information age" have adequate access to facts; but in regards to *Life* (*Spirit*-formed spirituality), witness and motivation are always welcome.

Eugene H. Peterson
James Houston Professor of Spiritual Theology
Regent College
Vancouver, B.C., Canada

A NECESSARY INTRODUCTION

1

LIFTING OUR EYES
TO THE HILLS

n the blazing month of October, six years ago, I caught my first salmon.

Fought four, in fact, landed two, and tossed one back to the water—all in a single day of fishing the Kenai River in Alaska.

The day was absolutely rinsed; its colors outrageously true, as though Alaskan air were a crystal lens; the wind so cold I could see my breath. My thumb on the wet reel ached. Morning and afternoon we stood in the boat, casting and cranking the line in, talking, marveling at the rushing abundant life in the river. It was like standing in an exaggeration, a cartoon, so many were the salmon jumping all around us.

At evening the sky deepened to purple-blue, and all the trees burned a cool, green-gold mystery. Still, we cast our lures midriver before us, cast our shadows back to the forests ashore.

This is how crowded the river was: the fish I returned had been hooked in its dorsal fin. One could almost snatch the salmon by dragging naked hooks among them. But it was an illegal catch, my friend said, and we set it free to spawn. "The fish has to *take* the lure," he said.

Well, the one which took and held my lure was a full fourteen pounds.

In the cold gloaming my knowledgeable friend, Paul Birner, cleaned this first catch of mine and cut it into pink steaks—thick, symmetrical steaks—which we grilled immediately. The ingredient the Midwest lacks for making salmon succulent is immediacy.

"You've got to see Denali," Paul said while we were eating. His wife and mine had joined us. We sat in a river cabin, close and warm.

Denali?

"Mount McKinley," he said. "Its native name is Denali, *the Great One.*"

Well, of course we would see Denali. How could anyone miss (I mean physically miss noticing) this highest peak on the North American continent? Nor was Paul the first to urge its grandeur upon us. Thanne and I planned to drive north from Anchorage to Fairbanks, right past the park that bore its name, Denali.

"The Park is closed already," another friend had said, a man who lived in Fairbanks. "But you'll come around a long bend in the highway, and suddenly the massive, white mountain will appear directly in front of you. Majestic! It'll take your breath away!"

Alaskans speak of Denali as though they stood in intimate, awe-full relationship with it. Even at great distances (even in their bathrooms, I suspect) they can point instinctively toward it—as oriented to the mountain as to their own hearts.

ᏩᎳᎧ

By the time we were fishing on the Kenai River, the lecture series that had brought me to Alaska in the first place was done. I had spoken to a gathering of pastors who served not-rich parishes; and since they hadn't the resources to pay me in money, they offered instead a vacation. That is, they loaned us a four-wheel drive pickup, lodgings wherever we wished to go, and all the sight-seeing they could barter from their parishioners. Thanne and I had a full week left for leisurely travel.

The timing in our private lives was perfect.

We had a significant decision to make: whether to move from our home of twenty years in order to accept a position at Valparaiso University. This would have to be the last move we made in our professional lives, if not in our lives altogether. Evansville was the hometown of our children, the only city they knew. Valparaiso was strange to them—and to us it would represent a complex commitment, just as I had fought free of external responsibilities in order to spend the rest of my days writing, writing, my pleasure and my one sure intent.

The decision required a wise response. But our wisdom is seldom sudden and never our own. Thanne and I required time to talk and not to talk; time to pray both silently and aloud, alone and together; time to allow the decision to grow naturally from a richer ground than our own. God *must* be that ground. And we (poor, unsteady children) need evidence that God indeed hears the plea, attends the process, and directs our deciding.

So we left our friends at the Kenai and drove away alone.

Time we had. Privacy we had. Answers we had not. No, answers we had none, despite all our praying. Ah, but Alaska has a slow magnificence—and we were not in a hurry.

৩৩৩৩৩

We drove south at first, to Homer, where we stayed at a true land's end, the very tip of a spit of land that reached out into cold Cook Inlet. Here was a wooden motel and stone and then sea. The sky was set afire at sunset. But God was not in the fire. We were living, it became apparent, in a restlessness like the rush and thunder of wave against rock.

Next we drove north to Anchorage, proud, clean city. We walked its long, woody paths. We went to the theatre. We talked together.

North. Again we drove north and north—but no Denali. Cloud covered that entire day of driving. And though we were able to see mountains, we could not define one singular majesty among them. It snowed lightly. This created an eerie beauty, for the hills and the valleys and the mountains beyond all were dressed in a darksome white, but the trees stayed black, and trestle bridges and the long train winding along its distant tracks, likewise, black. And the cold wind became perfectly still. And all the sky was indistinct, grey. The entire scene seemed to me an endless tracery, an etching of black on ivory in fine and private detail. Nevertheless, no Denali.

We laughed, Thanne and I. We said, "They're lying. There is no such mountain in Alaska."

> *O Lord, show us our going out and our coming in:*
> *what shall it be from this time forth, forevermore?*

In Fairbanks we met a bush pilot who said, "I'll prove the mountain exists."

So we flew up in a tiny red plane. We suffered the seclusion of a dense cloud cover for several minutes, then broke into a mist-white sky, flying south by southwest. Ed, the pilot beside me, is a taciturn fellow. Thanne, too, can be taciturn. Therefore we traveled each in our personal silence until Ed raised his hand and pointed.

As if through the whitewash of watercolor painting, the dim rosy shape of a faraway mountain had begun to form in front of us.

"Denali," Ed said.

And the mountain grew, surrounded by lesser attendant peaks. The mountain grew without changing posture or position or mood. Indifferent colossus! The mountain simply swelled before us. The mountain—and all else that rose above the cloud that covered the earth—became a dazzling white.

There was no earth upon which it stood. It had the strange quality of separation, an unreal air: muscles and up-juttings, all blinding white; terrible strength, pure white! Below us were the fixed flows of several glaciers. We flew at eleven thousand feet, and still we looked up at the mountain now filling the windshield: seventeen thousand feet at its peak. The mountain grew yet huger. I was not loving this titan exultant in its sky. I was fearing it. Ed told me to take the controls of the tiny plane. Immediately we dropped a thousand feet. Without a word he took over again.

Too much! Too mighty, too near, too massive, too white!

But now Ed was grinning. "Never been this close," he shouted. "Wind's light. Going closer."

I was gripping the seat between my legs, wondering where he would find the space in which to turn the plane around. White blocked us left and right. The mountain reached around us like the great arms of an easy chair. We were a mosquito in a mammoth's eye.

What if the mammoth blinks?

This was not Denali! This was Sinai with the smoke of God rolling round and round its stony peak—and I was

Israel, terrified of the thunderous voice of the Almighty, yearning to run backward. Let Ed go on alone. Let some other Moses speak for me. I was plain scared.

And Thanne had spoken nearly nothing the whole flight into the mouth of the mountain.

Suddenly Ed did turn. But he didn't need space left or right. He *dropped* into the turn, leaving my lungs behind us.

And suddenly the mountain vanished. I had not anticipated its complete departure—but there was no rear window in our tiny craft. All at once there was no mountain, as if it didn't exist—except that I continued to feel the tendons of fear in my neck.

This mountain was, it seemed to me, autonomous, transcendent and terrible. Let the Alaskans love it. I couldn't.

Where are you, O Lord? The psalmist says that you, our keeper, neither slumber nor sleep. But where are you now to speak to us?

෴

Two days later we had to leave Fairbanks. Our time had grown short. We had but a day and a half before flying home again. Therefore, under that persistent cloud cover, now become a serious snowstorm, we drove south on Highway 3. We had more than 350 miles to go that day—and now our trip had lost its leisure.

The highway was icy, the wind stiff, the drop-off steep on both sides, and civilization (it seemed to me) absent.

We were in wilderness alone, I was using four-wheel drive for the first time in my life, and the hills were growing steeper and steeper as we climbed into the mountain range. My wheels slipped and wallowed, and the hair on my neck stood up, and the snow blew blindness across the road, and I thought, *Who will find us when we roll down into the wood?*

I crept along at thirty-five miles per hour. Now and again a big truck roared by in scorn, raising clouds of loose snow. All my joints and muscles locked. My knuckles were white bone. Thanne said, "You're doing well, Wally. You're doing well."

I gritted my teeth. "I hate this," I whispered over and over. "I hate this."

And then, after seventy miles, this is what happened:

The white highway began to darken. Snow became mere powder on the air. Patchy blue sky appeared. My tires took hold, and my heart took comfort, and we stopped and got out and breathed, and we drove on, and the clouds broke up altogether, and then in Broad Pass an absolutely rinsed, outrageously blue sky spread around us as far as we could see—

—and there, to the southwest, was The Mountain, Denali, huger than any other, following us as other peaks passed on between us, *following* us, that mighty mountain, mighty and merciful now.

And Thanne began to cry.

"He was with us all the time," she whispered. "God was always with us, Wally. We just couldn't see him."

Now Denali was majesty indeed. There must have been a furious wind at the peak, since snow sheered south for several miles straight out through the blue air. It looked like white hair torn sideways; but it was so unutterably distant that the snow hung like a gentle veil upon the air.

I say "distant," but I was thinking, *close!* Because the mountain stayed with us now wherever we drove, leaning back and gazing toward heaven but moving in blessed assurance with us southward to Anchorage.

Even so had God been with Israel in the disasters of Egypt, in the holy storm at the Red Sea, in the wilderness day and night—and at Sinai when they feared that he had swallowed Moses and departed. Even so is the invisible Spirit with us still, everywhere and every-when. Even so is his very presence the consolation that answers prayer; for his presence *allows* us to decide according to our best intelligence; for there is no *where* we can go away from his Spirit. Whatever we choose, he chooses to go there with us, even if we should take the wings of the morning to dwell in the uttermost parts of the sea.

In Anchorage the following morning, still lying in bed, sunlight streaming in our window, we talked, Thanne and I.

Actually, Thanne talked. But her words were the same as the ones I was murmuring in my mind.

"It's okay, isn't it?" she said. "We can go to Valparaiso."

Can, she said. Not *must*. We were free.

"God is with us," she whispered again. "He never left us, Wally. He never will."

2

THE FOUR PARTS OF PRAYING

*P*rayer will never rust for want of use. People will pray.

There are so many terrors in the world that, spontaneously, they will pray. So much remains unknown; we have far more needs than we can meet, or even name, on our own; sickness and sorrow, hungers of mind and heart and body, anxieties and frights and nights and solitude—people will pray.

And moments of utter, unexpected beauty will draw an awkward thanksgiving. And sometimes our souls do groan with the sweetness of having been loved, which groaning Godward is a prayer: laughing, rejoicing, smiling, sighing—people will pray.

The meek-at-heart will by nature pray. But so will the tough one, the angry, the sentimentalist. And cynics and the streetwise and grandmas and fools and the faithful—all, all are of the failing flesh; all encounter mortality; all shall one day be less than their labor and their living requires; and all who love another truly shall suffer on behalf of their beloved. Today or tomorrow, the people will pray.

It may be long and lonesome. Or it may be one word spat between contemptuous teeth: *God!* It may be the contented murmuring of a familiar hymn, no words of my creating at all, but the words of my heritage and the serenity of my heart. No matter how, the people will pray.

But of all who pray, how many pray poorly?

How many, then, straightway dismiss this gift of God? How many grow restless over a period of time and despair of prayer—not because the thing itself is ineffectual, but rather because their practice of the thing is cheap and incomplete? Many. Oh, too many of the people turn their groaning inward (where it swells helplessly like an angry gas) rather than Godward (where the Deity himself breathes it in and transforms it).

What, then? If I, who never learned of computers in the first place, can't make a computer work, should I blame the computer?

If prayer seems like sand in my mouth, though the last I learned of prayer was in my childhood (or perhaps I've never learned anything of prayer *except* the spontaneous cries of childish weakness), should I scorn prayer? More absurdly, should I scorn those who do pray?

Of course not. I am both fair and a realist. I will not judge the thing I do not know, but will learn of it despite my seeming world-wisdom and my independence. And to learn of prayer is at the same time to learn faith. This learning begins with the mind and ends with the soul.

ဖေမာ

Prayer is a natural act. Even children know by instinct how to perform it with their parents. Nevertheless, it is more complex than many adults have had the patience to recognize. So the children prevail where their elders fail. I suspect that their unashamed dependency, their peaceful need of others' help for health and safety and daily life, makes them aware that prayer is not one act only: a cry unto God, words shot out of a hot need, words tendered gently to the Deity. The dependent child also watches and waits upon her parent in order to discover what will come next—and that rightly implies a second act, a third, and a fourth.

Simply, *prayer is communication*.

We talk *with* God, not just *to* him. God talks with us too, causing a circle to be whole and closed between us.

Complexly, the complete prayer is made up of four acts, four discrete parts, two of which are ours, two of which are God's. The parts may seem separated one from another by time or by the different nature of the acts; yet often all four acts occur in such swift succession that the complete prayer is revealed as a single, unbroken event. And so it is. It is communication:

—First, we speak,
—while, second, God listens.
—Third, God speaks,
—while, fourth, we listen.

If we initiate the first act, God will respond with the second. That is sure and certain. So is the third act absolutely certain to follow the first two, because God's love promises to speak to us by a Word.

But if we have never learned the fourth, if we are too impatient to perform the fourth act, too demanding and unsubmissive to watch and to wait upon the Lord, then we will never even know that the second and the third acts have been accomplished. Without our truly listening, prayer will seem to have failed because communication, remaining incomplete, *did* in fact fail. The circle stayed broken, and love was left unknown.

Learn the circle. Trust in God to listen and to speak, and our own listening will follow as easily as the eyes of a child follow her father—in whom is all her good.

1. We Speak

First (but only first) we speak to God.

The marvelous blessing is that we can, despite our insignificance, initiate this particular dialogue. We can trigger communication with God wherever, whenever, however our souls have need. Elsewhere in the world we must approach the powers according to *their* rules and readiness. Only when they are willing are we permitted audience. But with God our word alone makes readiness and a way. We are not summoned. We go.

And the merciful blessing is that any language works. We may talk as we are able; therefore, we are *made* able to talk this prayer. Ponderous religious phrases are fine. But so is lousy grammar fine. We may babble or roar or weep or sigh or put our foreheads against an old stone wall and wail. Fine!

And we may speak with any part of our beings: spoken words, surely, are fine; but physical gestures also communicate, kneeling, bowing, curling into a posture of helplessness, laughing out loud and clapping our hands. The soul alone may groan, soundlessly, feelings too deep for words. There may occur in our hearts a warm intensity of love, a holy suffusion of tenderness. These speak. This language works, so long as we turn—and know that we are turning—the self toward God thereby.

Godward: we speak *to God*. We do not merely mutter moods into the cosmos, putting our yearnings into words for the sake of expression alone. The act of speaking faces God; therefore, the act itself names God as clearly as we name the recipient of any message sent anywhere here below.

So Thanne and I were praying in Alaska, surely. By conscious words we laid our choices at the feet of the Almighty. More than that, even as we spoke with one another privately, struggling toward decision, our discussions were done in the hope of God's watchful presence. We laid *ourselves* at his feet, our mortal intelligence, our limited thinking. That was spiritual language Godward.

And our very driving through fresh country, aware that the Creator's invisible nature can be perceived in his creation, gave posture to our praying. Standing above an abundance of salmon, standing below the fiery sunsets of Homer, a playful and serious seeking for Denali—all this was a wordless bidding, as though we had entered a most holy Cathedral in order to stand before our God. All this was our talk, the first part of prayer.

2. God Listens

Let this be understood above all: the power of prayer is not in us, that we speak. It is in God, that he listens! It is his hearing that causes a true connection between us. The second act makes the first one possible.

When I was a child I thought I had to shout my prayers because God was nowhere in sight and therefore must be far away. I recall a particular night when I was lying in bed, in the dark, praying silently in my mind. Suddenly the thought occurred to me that the silent prayer was stuck within my skull, and I began to panic. How could God hear the soundless yearnings in a small kid's head? So I opened my mouth and began to mumble the prayer aloud. But doubt had planted its seed, and the next question was whether my baby mutterings could reach the Lord, sight unseen. Why, God was in heaven! And I lay far below on earth, in a house, in a small room in that house. So I shouted my prayer. I lay on my back and aimed my shout through the ceiling up to heaven. I *had* to. How else could God hear me?

On the other hand, I never shouted into the telephone, though my grandma was in another city and another state altogether. I never doubted that something else was responsible for carrying my voice through the wires to St. Louis, sight unseen.

So it is with God. God's love is the power that *receives* our voice. His near and windy Spirit gathers the prayer from its source and bears it to himself. This is God's promise. It is nothing we ourselves accomplish. We may be peaceful with the feeblest muttering, since the Spirit both searches the heart and intercedes.

So if children are silly enough to think their shouting must power the prayer to God, then adults are even sillier when they think their righteousness or their faith or some correct form of praying powers their prayers to God—as though they must make God listen! The weakest, most miserable sinner shall be heard for no other reason than this, that God chooses to hear prayer.

Thanne and I in Alaska, we were doing what comes naturally. As the snow falls simply because it is snow, so we uttered bafflement simply because we are people in whose nature it is to express ourselves. Likewise, as the earth catches the snow and gives it place and shape, a lodging for a while, so God was catching our various utterances, giving them shape and substance within his heart. Our scattered talk and our confusion found form in God—though we did not know what form until he turned it back to us again.

3. God Speaks

It is precisely at this point that people often cease their praying, assuming it to be accomplished. Having stated their demands, they attend to other things and wait delivery as if God were a mail-order company.

But the prayer itself is not yet done, and to think so is to cut it at the gut. If anyone stops here, he frustrates the event wholly and in consequence may find (false) grounds for scorning prayer itself.

The third part of a complete prayerful communication is that God now speaks to us. *Speaks* to us: this is not the same as giving us what we want, which he may or may not do hereafter. In love he responds. He talks back, answers, makes himself known, makes his being and his intentions real unto us—so that we who call may meet and recognize the listener to our call; so that we who love may know the object of our loving.

Except we wait for that, we are merely using God, reducing the Almighty to a candy machine whose only purpose is to respond when we punch its buttons, satisfying the hungers we define. But God is alive. He participates in conversation. His yearning is to be heard as well as to hear, to lead, to explain, to console, to solve and resolve not only our problems but our very *selves*, to satisfy not only the petty hungers we can name, but the deeper hungers only a Holy Father can identify.

And in what language will God speak to us? Well, he speaks as ever he spoke of old. All the elements of creation and all the details of human experience can be the elements of the divine response. The "words" of God are not confined to sounded or written symbols. God spoke to Israel by *acting* among the people. Most brightly, the Word of God was incarnate in Jesus, who *acted* the glory and the love of God among us. Immanuel: the suffering, death and resurrection of Jesus—*that* was the creating and re-creating Word loudly shouted within the world.

God speaks to us through the Scripture which records the actions of Jesus. And through the words of other people, both those who are faithful and those who are not. And through the Church, in which the Holy Spirit breathes truth. God can be very verbal in the mouths of others.

But the acting God speaks to us also in the stuff of our daily experience.

Do I write stories which contain a wisdom wiser than my own? Then God is speaking with acute evidences of the Spirit's presence in me: I did what I cannot do. God did it through me. God is here. My skill has become his instrument!

Have my children forgiven me when I didn't deserve it and their human capacities were far too limited for such a miracle? Have my children forgiven my sins against them when all the laws of this world and of personal survival required that they fear me, avoid me, or despise me outright? Yes, they have. Of their own nature, they could not—but they did. It is a paradox whose solution can only be this: that God forgave me *through* them. It is God's love speaking. It is God's word in my children for their wayward parent.

So part of the praying which Thanne and I did in Alaska—the third part, actually—was that dismal, persistent cloud. The weather was a genuine element of the communication with God: God's part. God's murmuring word, then, was a bush pilot's flight to the mountain's terrifying summit, a snowstorm, a sudden clearing of the heavens and the appearing of Denali itself massive and merciful on our own low ground: *Wally, he was with us all the time. We just couldn't see him.*

4. We Listen

And still (and still!) the sequence of communication is not complete until we have attended to the more difficult of our two acts. As God empowered our word by listening to it, so we manifest faith in him and dependence upon his word by listening to it.

How much love God lavishes on each particular heart when he murmurs words intended for that heart alone! How much love the lonely heart misses if it will not hear the personal word.

Only rarely does the Lord God speak in dreams. As it was in the days of Samuel, so it is today: open visions are very rare. And since God will not always shout for our attention, listening cannot be an accident. Listening must be our own conscientious action, a thing *we* do, a thing we *choose* to do, a thing we can learn to do better and better.

The Lakota Indians have said to their children: *Wachin ksapa yo!* It means "Be attentive." Have an attitude of constant awareness, for God may suddenly speak in any thing of his creation. If one is attuned to the marvelous complexity of the world, even the tiny steps of the ant can sound like drumbeats because they have become so heavy with meaning.

When the psalmist listens with a sacred attention to the various forms of nature, he can hear of the wonder of God. He hears a mighty and holy chorus, praising God. For creation, when it obediently does what the Creator commanded, both praises God and reflects the will of God: *Praise the Lord, all his angels!* cries that psalmist (148). *Praise him, sun and moon and all you shining stars! Praise the Lord from the earth, you sea monsters and all deeps!* And what else might reward our attentions, in whose beings we may hear God honored? *Fire and hail, snow and frost, stormy wind fulfilling God's command. Mountains—*

Yes, mountains. Yes, Denali, too.

But we hear first by making ourselves ready to hear, paying attention and genuinely trusting the Creator God to write his will upon the sea and the leaning tree. The anticipating heart! A faithful, Godward yearning, convinced that God neither abandons nor disappoints us. The child's sweet, perpetual sense of where her parents are moving, breathing, standing, loving: this is the first preparation to hearing the Lord speaking to us, our love of him and our faith in him.

Likewise, the apostle Paul declares that what may be known about God is plain to absolutely everyone in the world, "because God has shown it to them. Ever since the creation of the world his invisible nature, namely, his eternal power and deity, has been clearly perceived in the things that have been made" (Romans 1:19–20).

But it is immediately necessary for me to offer a caution and at the same time to indicate the second preparation for hearing the words of God within our experience. An attentive attitude is not enough if we don't know how to distinguish God's voice from other voices or how to interpret the voice of God when he does speak.

I said in the third part of prayer that God speaks to us through Scripture. The words of Scripture are ever the words of his present conversation with us, with each of us particularly. But they are, too, the words he has spoken of old; they record the deeds which constitute his manifold communications with humankind, his laws, his mercies, his judgments, his dear salvations. And more than the actual words of God, Scripture also interprets these words! It is in the Bible that we find our first and deepest explanations of what God's deeds *mean*. Deuteronomy interprets the act of Salvation which was God's leading the Children of Israel from Egypt to the Promised Land. The Prophets, likewise, interpret unto their ages (and unto ours) what the Word of God intends to say, to whisper, to demand. The Evangelists of the New Testament not only record the story of Christ's suffering, dying and rising again: they also grant us various teachings of the meaning of the cross. So does Paul in his epistles.

Do you see? The Bible is God's dictionary! It presents both his words, his chosen language (which has always been *action* among the people of the earth) and the meanings of those words.

To recognize the word of God in our own lives, then, it behooves us to know his language as recorded in the Bible. We must learn Scripture in order to distinguish God's voice from, say, the voices of our own yearnings! Even just to know *that* it is God talking—and not our strong desires, which can delude us after all—we must hear him speaking where we know for sure it is him: in the Bible.

And then, to know *what* the voice of God is saying, we must use the Holy Dictionary, comparing this present experience of God's communication with previous communications recorded in the Bible.

When someone we love dearly is sick unto death, we pray passionately for some kind of healing.

And then some small thing occurs: perhaps our beloved smiles in her sleep; perhaps a person of some religious reputation promises that she will get better; perhaps we dream that our beloved is radiant, swinging on a summer's swing. Upon that small thing, our strong desire may build an elaborate interpretation that God has said, "She will get well."

And then she dies.

Now we rush to reinterpret. Or else we grow furious with God, the Liar.

Or else we admit that we had not interpreted truly the voice of the Lord—if, indeed, these dreams were the word of God at all. It is so easy to assume a meaning that God did not intend. It is so easy to think we hear God on our right side, while he is whispering on our left.

The second preparation is an intellectual process: to grow ever more familiar with the Bible, daily to return to it and always to seek in *it* the meanings of God's acts today and tomorrow.

This brings us to our third preparation, which is our practice of personal, holy disciplines before God: the practice of specific pieties.

How can they hear whose ears are ringing with their own loud voices, their own cravings and fears and foolishness? Be silent!

Or, to show the path to silence, be humble before your God. Empty the self of self. Take upon yourself the posture of obedience, even before the thing which must be obeyed is even spoken: *obey the Lord in listening!*

"Ask," said the Lord to Solomon in a dream by night, "what I shall give you." Solomon loved the Lord. He did not ask for long life or riches. Rather, Solomon said, "Give your servant an understanding mind to govern your people, that I may discern between good and evil."

"An understanding mind" is really *a hearing heart*. Solomon's request, according to the Hebrew word he used, is for the ability *to hear and to obey*—both at once, for both acts are one act. Consider, too, that "heart" here means more than the seat of the intellect. *What*, within this praying king, inclined itself to the Lord in humility, in a listening obedience? Why, it was the very core of his being: intellect and will and emotions, that which makes the human human, that which makes this person distinct from all other persons. *How*, then, does wise Solomon wish to listen unto God? Why, *in his heart of hearts.*

This is the wisdom of King Solomon: that he desired to be wholly and completely obedient to the will of God in order to govern the people of God wisely and well.

Our own ability to listen improves as we mimic such humbleness with our own *hearing hearts.* This heart waits upon the Lord. This heart is capable of remaining both hopeful and empty until the Lord himself fills it. This heart does not reject words which the Lord may speak harshly! It does not limit the voice of God by limiting its listening, but will receive *whatever* the Lord chooses to say. It waits upon the Lord: that is, it is listening always, always. If Paul's injunction to "pray without ceasing" means anything common to the common person, it surely means to be listening without ceasing—since this fourth act of praying is as significant as the first act.

So we prepare ourselves by the pieties.

We will give alms because such giving affects our attitudes, our pride and our own poverty. We will tithe, yes, because it places all we have under the economy of God, and nothing can then be considered ours except by his providence. We will worship with a clockwork regularity, even when the preaching is dull and the least of that activity; and we will arrange our very weeks according to the Lord's mercy and desire, observing sacred rest in order to discover personal silences into which the voice of God may come. We will make a devotion of Scripture and a Scripture of our common utterance.

And so our very being becomes a listening thing.

Or why else did Thanne and I perceive the very same thing, wordlessly, in the beautiful word that the Lord God vouchsafed unto us in the days of our deciding? Perhaps it was fear that emptied me of myself, the profound recognition in that snowstorm that I am little and nothing on my own, that I will live only in dependence upon the greater God. And perhaps the fright of confronting the white mountain face-to-face in the sky made my future seem such a blank that I could do nothing *but* wait till the Lord began to fill it in. Perhaps the circumstances themselves were as humbling as any pieties I was in those days pursuing. Whatever the cause, I was listening. I was with my whole being attentive, personally ignorant, desperately seeking.

And so we heard, Thanne and I.

No, we didn't hear, "Yes! You must go to Valparaiso."

Nor did we hear, "No, don't go."

We heard, *I am with you. Whatever you choose, wherever you go, I will bless the endeavor. Worship me then as you have worshiped me here, seeking my face in Alaska, and I will be there with you—even when you cannot see me.*

3

THE CIRCLE OF WORD AND WORD AND LISTENING

ven children (*especially* children, since they are unashamed of their dependence upon the strength and the favor of others) pray in a full circle of communication.

"Help me!" they cry without complication. "Jesus, please come and help me!"

And because their need is always so great—ever a matter of life and death, of sorrow or salvation—children tune themselves to the voice of God with desperate intensity. God may speak in any language, then, because there is no language the child will not understand. Need gives them ears, and weakness gives them hearing. *Any port in a storm.* Any warmth in this cold world is warmth enough. Any word by which the Lord God chooses to ease their difficulty is God and the Lord indeed!

Why, they may hear comfort in the rocks themselves, and they shall not be wrong. They ask *trusting*. They manifest trust by *asking*. And trust presumes that God shall hear and, hearing, answer.

So, then, these two things—their admission of a complete personal need, and their complete trust in the alert mercy of the Heavenly Father—together make children adept at prayer. Need and trust, love and the conviction that they *are* loved: the circle is easy for children, and prayer is natural in their mouths.

In the late autumn of my thirteenth year, my mother decided that it was time for me to earn my way in the world.

"A paper route," she said.

We lived in Edmonton, Alberta, Canada. I was the eldest of seven children, a quiet, contemplative child of few evident skills. My brother played hockey and won public awards. I read books and lurked in my bedroom.

But Mom had already telephoned the *Edmonton Journal* on my behalf and had committed me to a newspaper delivery route near the edge of the city, Eighty-eighth Street and Eight-ninth, each five blocks long.

"The Polish live in that neighborhood," she said. "Be nice and they'll be nice to you. Wally—you will earn nine dollars a week. What do you think of that?"

I was almost persuaded. Nine dollars would make me solvent, a book-buyer of some authority.

Mom said, "I've opened a bank account for you. This will be your savings for college. See? You're already becoming a man."

Now, on the plains of western Canada autumn is winter already. Kids trick-or-treated in the snow. And when we left school in the midafternoon, it was already darkening toward night.

Working kids did not go straight home.

I met the fellow who was turning his paper route over to me and we walked to the "paper shack" where carriers received fresh newspapers for delivery. It was filled with boys bigger and louder than me, everyone at ease in the melee, shouting, laughing, punching.

The papers arrived in heavy, high stacks wrapped in offset cardboard and bound tightly in twine. Norm, the supervisor, snapped that twine with a violent finger-knife and counted out smaller bundles, crying: "Johnson, seventy-five! Yurka, sixty! Glettik, one hundred! Krause, fifty. Wangerin, a hundred and nineteen! Wangerin? Where's the new kid? Wangerin!"

Norm had the nose of a rooster and no upper lip. I wondered whether he could actually close his mouth. I raised my hand.

"Next time, jump!" he said. Then he said, "Look at you! You're smaller than a whistle. You sure you can carry these?"

A kid named Wayne said, "If not, he'll crack like a cock-a-roach."

To this day my mother says that the curvature of my spine is due to the load I bore daily from the paper shack to my route.

For a week the departing paperboy ran me up and down his old route. He commanded and I delivered.

"In the door!"

"This house never tips."

"Little yappy dog here. She'll bite your pant leg."

"Run, cock-a-roach! *Run!* You'll never get done in time. There's folks here'll call the *Journal* and complain if they don't get their paper before supper!"

On Thursday he delivered while I watched. Collection day: thirty-five cents a week. He had a route book in which he noted those who paid and those who didn't. Friday and Saturday he returned to the houses who owed him money. Then he gave me his route book and walked out of my life.

On Monday I was on my own.

It was dark when I started. I followed the route book assiduously, peering at it under the street lamps, running hard to the homes that received papers, creeping back to the dreary light to read again. It took me three hours to finish. My feet had frozen to a dull ache. There was no feeling left in my toes. I began to wonder how many Polish people were calling to complain. I didn't see anyone anywhere. Wilderness. On the north side of my route the streets dead-ended at a vast expanse of concrete, possibly a parking lot for eighteen-wheelers: the calculated emptiness struck dread into my heart as if this were more than the uninhabited edge of the city, as if I stood looking into the void of the universe.

"So, Wally," my mother said when I got home, "how does it feel to earn your own way? I guess we can allow a working man to skip supper. Once."

On Wednesday I forgot the route book. If panic is a sort of suffocation, I ceased to breathe. The child did not inhale the whole time he dashed the dark streets, trying to deliver the newspapers by memory. Sometimes he knocked to ask whether this house received the *Journal*. Mostly, he guessed. Then he walked home in misery because there were still six papers in his sack.

"So, Wally, do you feel like a man yet?"

On Thursday I stopped at every house to collect payment for papers received. "It's the paperboy!" I noted in my book a neat "35" by every name that paid me.

A thickset man came to the door in his undershirt, holding a dark drink in his hand, fizzing. "No paper, no money!" he said. "I see no paper yesterday, you got no money today. Where's the other boy? Who are you?"

The concrete space, that cosmic dearth at the edge of my route, seemed to be swelling, preparing to swallow me down into a windless solitude.

My mother said, "Young man, this is the fourth time you've come home late, and this is the last supper you will ever miss, do you hear me?"

Friday it snowed. The snow softened my step. It sifted into my sack between the papers. It touched my face with tiny ice. It silenced the whole world, causing in me an unspeakable loneliness.

But it was on Saturday that my soul was cast into the deepest pit of need, and I cried out unto my Heavenly Father for help.

༄

Every Saturday morning, paper carriers were required to take their collected monies uptown to the offices of the *Edmonton Journal,* there to give the company its due. This, I understood, was the transaction by which the newspaper survived. Upon the receipts of paperboys did a giant corporation stand. What was left over after our payment we got to keep, *our* due.

So I put forty dollars worth of change into a small cloth bag and went forth from my house and boarded the trolley bus that would transport me to the center of Edmonton. A bright, snow-sparkling day. Early winter. A nice sting to the boy's cheeks, cleanliness.

I glanced from the window of the bus. People were puffing clouds with their breathing, entering shops—

Suddenly I realized that I had no idea where to go in the huge complexity of the *Journal* building, what door, what floor, what window, what place, what person! My heart turned to wax and melted down into my stomach.

What if I didn't turn my money in? What then? I would be stealing! Oh, lost! And what could I possibly say to my mother? And so, should I even *go* to the paper shack on Monday? Norm and his violent little finger-knife!

The bus now was hurtling forward. No time to think! My face was on fire. Where would I get off?

"Help me," I whispered. "Dear Jesus, please come and help me!"

I meant that cry as surely as if I were dying and Jesus alone had life.

And then I sat rigid, exceedingly alert—a leaf that flutters to any shift in the wind.

Does God answer prayer?

The paper carrier named Wayne got on the bus. He had a face made pink by the weather and by his own compulsive humor.

"Cock-a-roach!" he said when he saw me. "So what did you collect this week?"

Is it coincidence that he sat down beside me? And went into the *Journal* building with me? Maybe, but that doesn't matter. Wayne was also, unequivocally, the voice of God.

By prayer I had reached toward God. By faith I *expected* my Heavenly Father to reach back. So my great need and my great trust heard the whispering of Almighty God in the laughter of a confident paperboy. Wayne said, "Well, I see you ain't cracked yet, Cock-a-roach."

But God said, *I love you. And I am always with you.*

1. The child cries out,
2. convinced that God is listening.
3. Therefore, when God answers,
4. the child hears in the smallest word the grandest proclamations of love.

෩

In the weeks that followed I walked my route in a goodly and genial company. Well, God was there.

And the thickset man who had withheld payment before now invited me in from the cold. "Want some-ut

46

to drink?" he said. He held up his glass of dark fluid. "Coke?" he said. "A swallow of rum and Coke?"

I grew to like the Poles. In time my mother told me that our veins, too, ran red with a Polish blood.

And I learned which houses had bathrooms in their basements; and I developed the confidence to use them.

Knock, knock! Who's in there?

Oh, it's just me, the paperboy.

And the black expanse along the northern border of my route became adventure, allowing my imagination its daily, wild romance: for I alone stood between civilization and the wilderness.

When I rang the doorbell, a yappy little dog came skidding round corners in the kitchen, in a furious rage to bite my pant leg; but the boy of that house became my friend and followed me while I worked because I could tell him stories.

And God was there. I had the proof. I had begun to dwell within the circle of his presence, wherein is comfort and purpose and life and love and confidence.

ONE

WE SPEAK

INTRODUCTION

"Jesus, help me!"

A child's completely spontaneous outburst, the cry that sends his need and his whole soul to God, that is prayer.

The more persistent and complex communication with which Thanne and I bent the ear of the Almighty in Alaska—because we had one urgent thing on our minds—that was prayer.

The mother who sees her son coming home after the snares and the perils of some youthful risk, who in a sudden rush of relief breathes, "Thank you, Jesus!"—she is praying.

One voice speaking for several hundred during worship—or several hundred voices joining in a single familiar formula: both are prayers.

Or what should restrict the forms of our praying? That which we speak toward God, that remains the valid and the first act of sacred communication no matter how long or short, how simple or how elaborate.

This is the first prayer my parents taught me: *Abba, Father, amen*. It was my infant expression of relationship. When I uttered these three words, I accomplished the first of the four parts of prayer. It was enough.

Nevertheless, as I grew up I learned the great variety of ways by which we may speak to God, or else my praying would be restricted by my own ignorance.

We are surrounded by a host of those whose grace it is to pray well! Psalmists, poets, martyrs, saints and witnesses, men and women of gentle faith, people of suffering and of joy. And what shall we do with their gifts?

It is no less a prayer if we take their words and make them our own, for one may build a beautiful house then give it away so that another one might live in it.

Or we may learn the manner and the form of the prayers others have prayed, then create our own prayers according to their patterns. In this case they shall teach us how to pray.

Again, we may observe the lives, the passions, the hearts of those who have prayed well and discover there why we ought to pray, and *when,* under what circumstances.

Or we may, as I do often, curl ourselves privately within the beautiful petitions of voices more angelic than ours and let their prayers themselves become the answers, the murmurings of the dear God unto us. Even so do I pray with Johann Sebastian Bach and John Wesley and John Newton and Gloria Ferguson, great-hearted beseecher of the congregation where I have been a pastor.

And Thanne: When my quiet wife prays, then I am silent, for I am praying, too.

4

PRAYING WITH THE PSALMIST

magine for a moment that the psalm is like a house already built and that you are invited to enter there to make it your own. Praying from within the psalm is to pray your own prayer after all; for though you use words already written, you have become the present and living soul within those words.

Surely, some benefit shall befall you if you merely repeat the psalmist's words; but repetition is a little like walking around the outside of the house, admiring it, taking its color and shape into *your* mind, into your mouth.

The psalm desires to take you into *its* rooms. It waits to be filled with your mind and your heart. And it offers you several different doors through which you might enter and abide there.

One such door is the door of learning and analysis. As we discover the various interpretations of Hebrew words, the psalm yields its deeper meanings to us. Likewise, knowing the culture in which the psalmist wrote, the methods of worship, the views of God, the land, the conventions of Hebrew verse: all these grant us entrance into the psalm.

But there is another door which doesn't require scholarship as much as it does the keen self-awareness of the one praying. This is the door of poetry and imagination. It opens to all who knock with genuine need, so that they may go in and pray the psalm as their own. This is the door I want to show you now.

For the simple entering in, I will use Psalm 23 as an example.

But once you are inside the house/poem you need not be static, standing still, speaking one thought only. You may move from room to room as characters in a play move from act to act, changing as they go. Within the guidance of the psalm, *you yourself may change in the praying*. It is as if you rise several levels, from the basement to the bright air of the living room.

Later, I'll use Psalm 130 to show you this blessed effect of praying with the psalmist.

Psalm 23

How does a poem work? It works *with* the reader. The reader and the poem complement each other. Like a man and a woman, they *complete* each other. The poem hints, suggests, implies—while the reader takes the hint, fills the suggestion with her own real experience, turns an implication into an open emotion and brings to life what had only lurked upon the page.

The poem invites the reader to uncover her own truth by telling her but half a truth, the other half of which is hers to find. That's the difficulty and the reward of poetry: it demands so much of the reader. It is not merely imparting information or knowledge. Rather, it wants the reader to fill its tiny frame with her *self*. But then it gives back to the reader that self, awakened and aware.

How does a psalm work? Among other things, the psalms are poems, and so they work as a poem works: *with* us, inviting us into the houses of themselves, presenting us with a part of a picture so that each one of us might imagine the rest from our own experience. Psalms shimmer into life, then, because they open themselves to *your* life.

When you pray them this way, then, they become a special kind of poetry, the meeting place where three lives twine into one. The psalmist, the poet, has left the hint behind him; you, the reader, by praying the psalm now breathe a present emotion into that hint; and the hint concerns the God of both, who inhabits the join between you two!

An ancient writer of the first utterance, a present voice praying, and God between: a union! The proper business of the poem-prayer.

∽∽∽∽

No, the Lord is *not* my shepherd. Neither am I a sheep. I am a man something over six feet when I stand up in socks (what sheep ever wore socks?), and my God is one whom I cannot directly describe at all. But *indi*rectly, by figures and bright fragments, the psalmist hints at his relationship to the Lord. I will honor his language completely, not forcing it to fit my own preconceptions (or else I would never enter *his* house at all; I would stay forever imprisoned within my own). But if I can finish his hint with my personal experience, then I not only come to understand his relationship to the Lord, I myself do enter there, and it becomes mine.

All right, then: I have seen sheep. I have watched these timorous creatures raise foolish faces to me as I walked down a country road skirting their green pasture. And what was my experience? I despised them. I wanted to run at them and throw them into a confusion simply because they were so wretchedly dependent, so vulnerable, so helpless!

In those days I was a graduate student both arrogant and broken, both proud and so defeated that I knew not where to turn any more. I had entered the masters program for English literature convinced that all I needed for survival and success was my own intellect, my marvelous self! I saw no need for God. God, to me, was the Infinite Other, the source of all existence, surely, but not a personal being who might know me, whom I might know. No need, then, to supplicate the Mysterium Tremendum, the Big Secret. I trusted in myself.

And though I did well at first, I began to suffer a loneliness so deep that there were no words for it. I didn't make the connection. I just felt sad. Near the end of my first year in graduate school the loneliness became debilitation. It so consumed my heart that I couldn't pay pure attention to my teaching or my studies. I began to lack even the simple ability to deal with small pains. When I cracked my head on the corner of a kitchen cabinet, it was enough to make me cry. Loneliness had become abandonment.

I tried to heal myself by rushing to friends in other cities, but this was always unsatisfying, because my friends all had their own lives. And besides, the dread in me refused to be explained. There were no words for it.

Finally, I went to Dr. Spiro Peterson, dean of the graduate school. I had four papers due as well as oral exams for the M.A. I could neither think straight nor write a line of prose.

So I sat in Peterson's office and asked whether I might take incompletes in all my courses and still keep my fellowship.

He asked me why such extraordinary measures were necessary.

To my own surprise, I blurted out: "I'm having trouble with God."

He sat still awhile, considered my question, I thought. Then, gently, he said, "I'm sorry. No."

I burst into tears. My last recourse had been taken away.

I walked out of his office, across campus, through the tiny town and into the country—

—and there were those imbecile sheep! Whey-faced, blinking idiots! Nonentities, stupid, stupid! I wanted to scream at them, to prove what fools these sheep be.

But I didn't. Just as I turned toward the flock, a farmer emerged from the timber behind them. A man in coveralls and a John Deere hat, he clucked twice. Immediately every sheep was oblivious of me. They turned and began strolling to the farmer, who had himself turned back into the wood—and I was left on the country road alone.

For the second time that day I let my tears come. Oh, how I wanted the peace of these sheep! Dear God, I wish someone would relieve me of deciding and doing, of responsibility and the desperate diffusion of this life! Just come and whistle. Give me your *self,* O Lord, as my single focus and all my thought, and I will in great relief follow you!

Lord, be my shepherd, and I shall not want!

That same day I returned to my apartment with this one thought in my mind: "It doesn't matter. I don't *have* to achieve. I will do what I can do—and I'll leave the rest to the Shepherd. Jesus, I hold you to your word: *I am the Good Shepherd.* As for me, I am done with worrying. I am done with this failing effort to be my own guide, dependent on none by my own self only."

It is no coincidence that I was able, thereafter, to write my four papers. As soon as I was no longer my own creator; as soon as my classwork diminished again to its proper importance; as soon as I relaxed into the pastures of my Lord, my native gifts (gifts, indeed, from my Lord) were free to accomplish what God had intended for them.

> *He maketh me to lie down in green pastures:*
> *He leadeth me beside the still waters.*
> *He restoreth my soul:*
> *he leadeth me in the paths of righteousness*
> *for his name's sake.*

No, I am not a sheep. But I have been like a sheep. And though the Lord is in fact no shepherd, he is like that farmer of my experience. Out of the trees he comes walking and calling, and because of him I am safe and able and foolish and wise all at once.

In this way the psalmist's hint comes fully alive: the picture embraces us both (his conceiving, my experience), and the relationship he presents is resurrected again between the Lord and me! You, too, may read every metaphor and simile in the light of your own experience. No figure of speech works well until you permit your life to dwell in it.

> *The valley . . . of the shadow . . . of death.*

Who has not suffered so deeply that the darkness of his pain is the darkness of death? This passage seems immediately to speak of dangers, sorrows, fears and dyings. Nevertheless, when you pray this passage do not neglect the simple picture by which the psalmist moves *toward* the word of comfort in the midst of suffering. First fill the sense-image with your experience.

Have you been in mountain valleys? There the sun may suddenly drop away. Has the descent of night ever frightened you by its cruel speed? What about the trackless woods? Have you ever lost direction in the grim wood and grown panicky as time passed and your efforts seemed only to take you farther and farther away from civilization? To the child lost, trees become knobby demons, animals giggle and growl, and the good world is transfigured into a dark valley, threatening and wicked.

Can you recall those darknesses wherein you were finally and fully convinced that death must follow all of this? *That's* the darkness the psalmist/poet presents. The darkness of an endless night when you sat with someone beloved and very sick? Yes. The darkness of imprisonment? Yes. The darkness of the sleeplessness of divorce? The darkness of the night before your own surgery? Yes, yes! You are moving from the physical sensations of darkness to the spiritual experience. First the image/imagination, and then the deeper meanings of the soul.

Now, read with real astonishment the next portion of your prayer where, even inside such dreadful darknesses, you

> *fear no evil;*
> *for thou art with me;*
> *thy rod and thy staff,*
> *they comfort me.*

This very personal word of faith arises best in the worst of sufferings! The rod disciplines. The rod strikes down everything that might hurt you. So what is it you feared? What enemy lurked in your deepest darkness? The shepherd defeats that very thing! And the staff catches you and keeps you from falling. No, you shall not slip into despair, nor into the perfect solitude of dying, no! If you've felt again and truly your remembered sufferings, then you shall feel as well the catch of the crook around your spirit, drawing you back to the Lord again. This is prayer, both spoken and answered at the same time! This is relationship in praying. It does not require the learning of theologians, just the honesty of human experience.

And what is your memory of tables set especially for you? Birthday parties? An anniversary when your spouse had none but you in mind, you only? Graduation? Retirement? The common evening supper with those you love? Thanksgiving dinners? What memories of love and favor does a meal call to mind? What memories of homely safety and trust and a filling satisfaction? Allow yourself (in the place of imagining) to feel these experiences again, and you will not only understand the psalmist's quick bit of a thought, but you will also sing with genuine feeling the grateful metaphor:

My cup runneth over.

No one can define heaven. It's too far beyond us. Yet the last figure in the psalm can quicken our feeling of what it means to be directly in the Lord's presence.

No, "presence" is too weak a word. But "house" abounds with strong associations. My mother's house, cleansed in springtime, warm in winter, rich with cinnamon smells in the autumn. My grandmother's house, lacey and over-stuffed and welcoming.

Surely goodness and mercy shall follow me
all the days of my life:

and I will dwell in the house of the LORD
  for ever.

Psalm 130

Once inside the house/psalm it is possible to experience the remarkable *dramatic* quality of these prayers. The tone, the voice, the mood at the beginning of the psalm often changes in the middle, becoming something new by the end.

If, by finding our own experience in the figures of the psalm, we have already made that voice our own, then we are the ones who change. Our spirits are washed, made new, lifted up.

Here, then, is a wonder of intense, complete communication! For even as we speak to God by means of the psalm, God not only listens but immediately speaks back to us through the selfsame (holy!) words of that psalm: *he* is the one leading us, changing us. And if we remain alert; if we do not bellow the prayer in self-pity or self-centeredness; if we have humility enough to recognize and to admit the sweet transfiguration of our own spirits by means of the prayer which we are uttering—why, then the fourth act of communication shall also have taken place, and the house/psalm shall be a home indeed.

ᏩᎠᎠᎥ

Who is so low that down looks like up to him?

Who suffers such depths of despair that she feels estranged from God?

Who thinks that God cannot or will not hear him when he cries out from the deeps of sin and willful rejection?

Or how deep down can deep be?
Listen to the psalmist:

Out of the depths have I cried unto thee O LORD!

"Depths" is the Hebrew word *tehom*. It is the same word used in the first verses of Genesis: "And darkness was upon the face of *the deep*." The word represents primeval chaos. It is like a cold, dark water so turbulent and wild and bewildering, that it refuses order and seems untouched by the hand of God. This "deep" is what was before God made anything to be.

These depths are the uttermost of nothingness. To be here is to be in doubt of any stable thing, any green thing, any dear or loving thing: it is to doubt life itself, since these depths precede creation.

Do you recognize the horror of such separation? Does it seem the end to you—that after which nothing else can come?

Even so, "the depths" is used in the Old Testament to describe the cold, cold river that runs at the bottom of "Sheol"—and Sheol is the pit into which the dead are thought to sink. Consider, then, a gorge so deep in the earth that nothing can go deeper. Imagine a crack in creation whose chasm the sun can never reach. In the deepest regions of that crack there flows a blind and frozen water: *tehom*.

From such a solitude, from such a desolation, from such a hell the psalmist roars to God:

Lord, hear my voice:
let thine ears be attentive
to the voice of my supplications.

And you, now praying this psalm so many years later: if the psalmist roars to God, you may do so too. Roar!

There is sin in this deep pit. Admit that. Sinning opened the earth beneath your feet, whether it was your sin or that of someone close to you, so you are suffering either guilt or a great and speechless grief. What was the sin that caused this gulf between you and the goodness of God? Can you speak it? Then speak it. For sin in its namelessness makes us afraid: it remains greater than our pitiful strength. And it causes in us the righteous dread that God will never listen to us again.

In order not to deceive yourself about your state, say with the psalmist:

> *If thou, LORD, shouldest mark iniquities,*
> *O Lord, who shall stand?*

That is the very core of terror. By sin my spouse or my child or my own poor self should be crushed, and then death is death for sure and forever, and we must grieve the deepest sorrow: that we deserve all we suffer. We belong in *tehom.*

Yet once you have truly (truly, specifically and humbly) identified the sin, the next phrase of your prayer can crack your darkness with a blinding flash of hope. Only to sin do the next words speak, but to sin they most certainly do speak:

> *But there is forgiveness with thee,*
> *that thou mayest be feared.*

This is the supernal nature of the Diety, the "what" that is God before us: he forgives.

And in speaking this shining declaration, you express your profoundest faith, even while God acts within the prayerful phrase and fills that faith with reality: he forgives. God abolishes the sin that caused your chaos and dropped you into the depths. There is no word more beautiful, nor any word truer: he forgives.

That thou mayest be feared, the psalmist says, because God's forgiveness is not a whitewashing of transgression, a sentimental wink at sin, a pat on the head. No, God's forgiveness first means that God saw in perfect detail what your sin was (such scorching scrutiny scares you a while). God's forgiveness knows exactly what it forgives, knows exactly what your sentence ought to be; and you (praying this prayer) know that God in righteousness could have executed that sentence—but he chose not to!

That thou mayest be feared. It means that sin is very strong. You have felt its power. But God is stronger. And in forgiveness you feel his even more terrible strength. But it is a strength on your behalf! So you stand in awe of the God who *chose* to overcome sin. Nothing, not anything in all creation, not the horror of your despair nor the troubles of those you love—nothing is mightier than God. One must fear such might. But one may at the same time put an absolute faith in it.

The psalmist does.

It is faith in the mighty goodness of God that permits the psalmist, in perfect confidence, to wait until God chooses also to act. The psalmist *knows* that it shall be; therefore his wait is no longer a desperate thing, but a yearning assurance:

> *I wait for the LORD, my soul doth wait,*
> *and in his word do I hope.*

Hope makes the waiting possible. The God who forgives will also deliver you from your troubles. You have the word even before you have the act. It shall be. Even in the midst of trouble, then, you are growing stronger. You yourself *are* strength for those around you.

Nevertheless, you wait with a jumping hunger, staring at the dark sky, waiting for the streaks of dawn which shall surely destroy this darkness.

The Hebrew word for "hope" contains a fierce element of tension between hoping for a thing and possessing it. So you pray your present state out loud in the words of the psalm:

> *My soul waiteth for the Lord*
>   *more than they that watch for the morning:*
>   *I say, more than they that watch for the morning.*

Lo, you have become the guards, the watchers in the night, those upon whom a city or a traveling band of pilgrims depends! You are, in your faith, no longer merely useless. No: you who pray become an answer to the prayers of others! In God, you are what you seek. You are the sentinel unto whom your beloved looks, while you look to the sky, awaiting God.

Have you by praying changed, then, you who were down so low? Do you see how the prayer is sometimes the drama of its own answer?

Do you see that, although *tehom,* the cold and the dark, may continue a while, yet your word was heard, your sin confessed, that sin forgiven, your God proven potent in forgiveness, and your faith made bright and mighty in witnessing God's forgiveness unto others?

That dramatic praying, spiritual though it is, shall materially change your affairs. And if you have, indeed, moved through the psalmist's stages from sin to trust, you will also understand the last word—which calls you to be active in this manifest changing of your affairs.

For it is you, now, who can urge the people around you to hope. With the psalmist your prayer may end in blessing and a clarion call to all whom you love:

O Israel, hope in the LORD!
  For with the LORD there is steadfast love,
  and with him is plenteous redemption.
And he shall redeem Israel
  from all his iniquities.
        Amen.

5

PRAYING WITH
THE FAITHFUL

hroughout history a gracious God has gifted certain men and women with the golden voice of praying. And because their prayers were so purely *right* for humankind in general, humans preserved them, praying the same prayers over and over—until they became the warp and woof of the devout language of the Church.

It is a treasure they have left behind. They grant us tongues with which ourselves to pray! They invite us to join an unbroken chorus, so that our small praying weaves us into the grand tapestry of the entire Christian Church, and we—though each remains an individual—are no longer merely one, no longer solitary. The prayer *is* our participation in a mighty choir.

These, then, are the invisible blessings of praying old prayers: they are a language we ourselves may not be able to discover and speak on our own; they were uttered first by people gifted of God; old prayers, therefore, may be more *right* for a need or an occasion than we, who are still stumbling through that occasion, have the wit to know; they have been polished to beauty and precision by the mouths of countless supplicants before us; they make each humble one of us members of a timeless and marvelous company. Our whispered petitions becomes sonorous music in the ears of God—and not one of us is left alone.

In our small study I can only touch upon several *kinds* of old prayers. The prayers of faithful people are literally innumerable. But you already know many of them yourselves—and perhaps many more than you might first suppose.

Let me encourage you to keep a "Commonplace Book" for prayers. It is itself an old tradition, a way of saving beautiful prayers for yourself by writing them down as you find them. This book will become very precious to you.

For each brief example below, I encourage you to add your own prayers—and so your book shall begin to fill with jewels.

Worship Prayers

Here is a prayer of jubilation and praise, a glorification of God's majesty and a glad confession of the divinity of Jesus Christ: the *Gloria in Excelsis*, "Glory to God in the highest." Its earliest known form dates from the fourth century, though it is probably older than that.

You will see how much this prayer draws its language from Holy Scripture, weaving many names and expressions for Christ into a seamless acclamation. Even so do the ancient prayers of earnest devotion find utterance first by a sweet obedience to the writings of the Apostles and Evangelists. (Just as songwriters today often prefer to set passages of the Bible to music that we all may sing them.) This old prayer, prayed today, joins us through ages and ages to those who first rejoiced in Jesus!

In its original use the *Gloria in Excelsis* was a "private psalm," sung in the morning office by small worshiping groups. It was probably introduced to the larger worship of the Church for the Christmas Vigil—the service on

Christmas Eve—because it rejoices in the incarnation of Christ. About A.D. 500 it began to be sung every Sunday by the leaders of the worship service. Since the eleventh century the opening phrase had been chanted by the worship leader, and all the rest sung heartily by the choir and then the people. As one man said: "Because the angel also began this alone, and then the whole army of the heavenly host sang it all together."

Here it is in a recent translation:

Glory to God in the highest!

And peace to his people on earth.
Lord God, heavenly king, almighty God and Father;
We worship you, we give you thanks, we praise you for
*   your glory.*

Lord Jesus Christ, only Son of the Father, O Lord
*   God, Lamb of God:*
You take away the sin of the world; have mercy on us.
You are seated at the right hand of the Father;
*   receive our prayer.*
For you alone are the Holy One, you alone are the
*   Lord, you alone are the Most High,*
Jesus Christ, with the Holy Spirit, in the glory of
*   God the Father.*
Amen.

Daily Prayers

Sometime after I had learned my baby prayer of trust, *Abba, Father, amen*—but earlier than I can remember— my parents began to pray two others prayers with me, one in the morning and one in the evening. They entered my soul about the same time as summer sunlight grew meaningful to me, the same time as midnight thunderstorms awoke me to terrors. These two prayers are as elemental in me as dawning and darkness. They shaped my days!

And they are about five hundred years old.

My father was a Lutheran pastor. It is natural that he should stand within that tradition particularly, and use for the intimate devotions of his family the prayers first written by Martin Luther.

Now, Dad could also pray with faith and force the prayers of his own heart, and he did. We, too, at bedtime lisped our spontaneous pleas to the Almighty and to Jesus. These prayers fulfilled their immediate purposes, then vanished with darkness and sleep.

But the regularly repeated prayers—they gave structure and shape to the rest of our devotion. And when we prayed them, we *all* as equals bowed our heads in an evident obedience to sacred measures larger than ourselves. This is important: both parents and children, by obedience, acknowledged the Holy Church to be larger than our sole selves; and by the same obedience I learned and also took the proper stance of prayer before God himself—faithful trust and humility!

Here is the morning prayer, still in the language by which I learned it. We prayed in the kitchen before children dashed off to school:

> *I thank thee, my heavenly Father, through Jesus Christ, thy dear Son, that thou hast kept me this night from all harm and danger; and I pray thee that thou wouldst keep me this day also from sin and every evil, that all my doings and life may please thee. For into thy hands I commend myself, my body and soul, and all things. Let thy holy angel be with me, that the*

wicked foe may have no power over me.
Amen.

Ah, what a comfort those words were for me! More accurate and more comprehensive than any I could have created for myself. I drew upon the wisdom of my elders in order to pray my prayer, and therefore the prayer itself embraced me with a godly consolation the whole day through. Now, I knew about evil, and I had suspected that a wicked foe existed. But because the old and honorable language of my elders also named these things, my infant fears were confirmed, and I found myself immediately in good company as we together stood in the strength of Jesus against them.

So I learned in an old prayer not only how to ask but how to thank. You *begin* with thanks. And you end with God all the day long.

Come the evening, then, when the children of Walter and Virginia were put to bed, when the dirty day had been bathed away, we prayed again, baby bursts of beggings and blessings, the Lord's own prayer as mighty and rhythmic as a tolling bell—and finally Luther's evening prayer to shape our day from sunlight to darkness:

> *I thank thee, my heavenly Father, through Jesus*
> *Christ, thy dear Son, that thou hast graciously*
> *kept me this day; and I pray thee that thou*
> *wouldst forgive me all my sins where I have done*
> *wrong, and graciously keep me this night. For into*
> *thy hands I commend myself, my body and soul,*
> *and all things. Let thy holy angel be with me, that*
> *the wicked foe may have no power over me.*
> *Amen.*

Now that I myself have grown older I delight in the knowledge that Luther also drew his prayers from the language of Holy Scripture. In fact, it was Jesus who gave such profound meaning to the phrase *Father, into thy hands I commend my spirit.* He prayed the brief prayer immediately before he gave up that spirit in death (Luke 23:46). But how much more wonderful it is to discover the actual trust in his last little prayer: for in Jesus' day those very words were used by little children in the evening, tucked into bed, just before they fell asleep. (See Psalm 31:5.)

Little children have, throughout the ages, sensed the association between falling asleep and dying. It's why they want night-lights. Saint Paul saw the connection, too— turning the deaths of those who died in the faith into "sleeps" from which the Faithful awaken. Such a close connection requires a prayer of confidence and love, and a listening God who loves and listens in return. This is the grace and necessity of "goodnight" praying.

Jesus knew. Jesus, the child of God, fell into his own death with this same childlike confidence.

And even so does the ancient prayer become blessed and contemporary when a little Wally-voice murmurs, *Into thy hands I commend myself,* and falls asleep one more night in peace.

Occasional Prayers

These are prayers composed for specific occasions, events, or experiences of significance which do not recur with regularity.

How shall we pray at the birth of a baby? Or at a wedding, how shall speechless gladness find its voice? What most accurate and satisfying word shall interpret our hearts when someone is sick unto death? And when they *do* die, what can give expression to the groaning and the mute questions within us?

Yes, as long as it is offered unto God the groan itself can become our prayer, for the Spirit intercedes for us with sighs too deep for words, and God, who searches our hearts, knows what is the mind of the Spirit (Romans 8:26–27). But poets of the past, those whom God has given the gift of skillful language, can turn groaning into an articulation of a devestating authenticity. That language can release the genuine complexity of our hearts, unlocking our own tongues, since groaning, finally, is an unexamined pain; it is the pain only, and not all that we would actually wish to *say* to God.

I will offer two examples of prayers whose beauty is in their passion and accuracy, both by Christian poets who wrote in England in the seventeenth century.

༄

The first occasion here to receive utterance in poetic praying is that of sickness and the approach of one's own death.

In 1623 the London preacher and poet John Donne suffered a disease so nearly fatal that he thought he might never rise from it again. Day by day he wrote a passionate series of devotions which were, in fact, a dialogue between himself and his God. They were the meditations of a man existing at life's extremities, the final journey from which there could be no returning. He expected to die.

In this state, Dr. Donne produced a prayer—a hymn, really—of remarkable appeal and simplicity. He was fearfully conscious of his sinning and of the disaster it *could* cause at the end of his days; but he was also certain of the forgiveness he had in Jesus. He took neither his sin

73

nor the Lord's grace for granted. Instead, he moved dramatically from the one to the other in this prayer, even as we must *move* into grace.

I, the night before a doctor opened my chest in order to remove a good portion of my lung, found this prayer to be precisely the sentiment of my soul—and I prayed it as my own:

A Hymn to God the Father

Wilt thou forgive that sin where I begun,
  Which is my sin, though it were done before?
Wilt thou forgive those sins through which I run
  And do run still, though still I do deplore?
    When thou hast done, thou hast not done,
      For I have more.

Wilt thou forgive that sin by which I've won
  Others to sin, and made my sin their door?
Wilt thou forgive that sin which I did shun
  A year or two, but wallowed in a score?
    When thou hast done, thou hast not done,
      For I have more.

I have a sin of fear, that when I have spun
  My last thread I shall perish on the shore;
Swear by thy self, that at my death thy Son
  Shall shine as he shines now, and heretofore!
    And, having done that, thou hast done,
      I fear no more.

Over and over I prayed that prayer, facing directly my sin and finding beyond that the doings of my dear Lord Jesus on my behalf, so that I could confront fearlessly the possibility of dying after all.

And somewhere in my breathing through Donne's prayer, I noticed the quiet introduction of his own name, twice saying, "thou has not [John] Donne, for I have more"—until the Son of God shines, and "thou hast [John] Donne," who is able to be in the arms of the Savior, just because he fears no more.

ᏫᎠᏁᎾ

The second occasion for which I have a sample prayer is Easter Sunday itself! But George Herbert uses the event of Christ's resurrection to embrace as well the physical and spiritual decay of our fearful sinning, the death we should have died, and the righteous supplication we may make to Jesus to lift us also up in his rising again.

George Herbert described his poems as "a picture of the many spiritual conflicts that have passed between God and my soul, before I could subject mine to the will of Jesus, my Master, in whose service I have now found perfect freedom." They were not published until after he died one month shy of his fortieth birthday.

Here, then, is a beautiful begging: that the once-for-all resurrection of Jesus should repeat itself in fact, in truth, in personal experience also in *our* lives.

Easter Wings

Lord, who createdst man in wealth and store,
Though foolishly he lost the same,
Decaying more and more
Till he became
Most poor:
With thee
O let me rise
As larks, harmoniously,
And sing this day thy victories:
Then shall the fall further the flight in me.

My tender age in sorrow did begin;
And still with sickness and shame
Thou didst so punish sin
That I became
Most thin.
With thee
Let me combine,
And feel this day thy victory;
For if I imp my wing on thine,
Affliction shall advance the flight in me.

A prayer like this can be endlessly revealing, new every time we pray it. Do you see the prodigal son lurking in its storied details? And surely the comparison of Christ's resurrection to the flight of a bird gives us a real picture by which to experience that magnificent day of divine revelation. "Then shall the *fall* further the flight in me!" What a wonderful reversal Jesus has worked upon our *fall* into sin: as deep down as we went, even so high and higher shall we fly!

And those through whom God has blessed the whole Christian Church with song and prayer—why, they are like the angels round about the throne of heaven, the number of them ten thousand times ten thousand and thousands of thousands.

We do not lack for words by which to utter every sentiment of the human soul, every need and every joyful cry of thanksgiving.

6

PRAYING IN THE FIVE-FOLD
FORM OF THE COLLECT

For more than fifteen hundred years a particular kind of prayer has been prayed during worship on the Lord's Day, a prayer that expresses the "collected" thought of an entire congregation with grace and brevity. In fact, it is called the Collect. We have and we continue to use hundreds of collects, ancient and modern. Their humility of spirit is balanced by certainty of faith. They span the full breadth of human need. They are filled with the goodness of the Gospel and with a constant sense of the support and the presence of the whole community of Christians.

The perfect collect is both strong and beautiful. It comes in the easy language of common people, but it is shaped by a wise and teaching *form*.

It is this form which can guide us also into a wisdom of faithful praying.

Many of us have learned to pray spontaneous prayers of supplication and thanksgiving. We pray the words that spring immediately to our lips: need shapes them, or the mood of the moment, or overwhelming feeling. Surely, this is our speaking unto God. It is righteous prayer.

But over time we may discover that our personal praying has fallen into a narrow rut of repetition, that our prayer-thought and our words are in fact more limited than our faith and our love, that we have so much more to *say* to God than our prayers are capable of containing.

Christian, have you paid attention lately to the focus of your prayers? Do you center mostly upon yourself?—what you need?—what you hope for?—what you desire (even lovingly) for those around you? Well, but there are *two* engaged in this communication. God is the other. Does God *as God* receive as much attention and detail as you grant yourself in your prayer? Do your topics of conversation relate mostly to the little you, neglecting the endlessly various Lord, about whom so much can be said?

Then learn the form which our wise forebears in the faith developed.

Use your own words! It shall in every respect be your speech unto the dear Lord God. But as you honor and obey the five separate parts of the Collect, you will (1) turn spontaneous cries into serious and thoughtful conversation with God, (2) find your attention drawn more and more to the very source and life of your faith and praying and (3) discover such a richness of petition that it *will* be capable of expressing the true complexity of your heart and mind.

∾

Here is an example of a very old collect, this one praying for our purity before the Lord. I will divide it according to its five parts so that you might see how seamlessly one leads into the next:

| *Invocation* | Almighty God, |
| *Basis for petition* | unto whom all hearts are open, all desires known, and from whom no secrets are hid: |

Petition	Cleanse the thoughts of our hearts by the inspiration of your Holy Spirit,
Purpose	that we may perfectly love you and worthily magnify your holy name;
Ending	through Jesus Christ, your Son, our Lord. Amen.

Any prayer on any occassion—whether private or familial or public—can be prayed according to these parts, and the one praying shall be moved farther and farther from self, closer and closer to God.

The Invocation

How important it is to name the one unto whom we speak, so that our prayer is not a monologue, a little internal speech, *about* God, or else merely in the vicinity of God. Conversation is dialogue. It exists only in its "between-ness," in the place where we and God meet and acknowledge each other.

But God has a multitude of names! And each one touches upon a different characteristic of his multitudinous relationship with us. Call him "Father," indeed. Jesus granted us this marvelously intimate title. But if we call him "Father" only, our actual approach to him shall be severely limited. Call him "Almighty" too. Call him "Everlasting," and "Merciful," "Creator," "Spirit of Truth," "Comforter," "Savior," "Master." Yes, all the names for Jesus might be used, as well as those referring to the Holy Spirit.

In fact, choose that name which, by God's own promises, contains that part of his holiness which is able to hear and to grant the particular petition which this prayer is about to ask.

Discriminate among all the names and titles of our God, and our God will grow larger and larger in your heart, and already your praying will break free of its old ruts.

The Basis for the Petition

Wait! Wait, wait—do not immediately rush to your request (which must needs center on *this* side of the dialogue), but rather consider God a little while longer!

The basis for anything that we could ever ask of God lies not in ourselves but in God! The assurance that our request is right; the assurance, further, that something can truly be done about it—assurances of any sort arise from God:

—From the nature of God, who he is;
—From the deeds of God:
    what he has done to reveal himself,
    what he has done and can do again for us,
    what marvelous deeds of his still echo in the world a power that now can fulfill our petition;

—From the promises made by God;
—From the teaching of God, his explicit commands and callings unto us.

In this second part of your prayer, then, speak out loud that which in God makes the petition appropriate and well within his power.

This will become your personal declaration of faith and certitude.

Let's say, for example, that a farmer is praying for rain.

He might begin, "O Creator and Sustainer of the universe," and then he might continue by lifting up before God these words: "unto whom all creatures look for their food in due season. . . ." His second phrase is his faith: *Lord, I have the right to ask this; and I know you, I believe in you, for you have accomplished my petition in the past.* His "basis" comes directly from Psalm 104:27. Holy Scriptures themselves empower the farmer's heart; the entire Psalm 104 assures him that God cares about the rain, the seasons, the harvest and the feeding of his people.

You see? The collect form of prayer requires a growing knowledge of God; but it is also grounded in God; and it holds God to his own promises with a boldness only the truly trustful can exhibit.

Therefore this prayer becomes a word of ours to God based upon a word of God to us. Conversation.

The first three parts of the collect appear already in the prayer of the disciples in Acts 1:24: "And they prayed and said, [1] *Lord,* [2] *who knowest the hearts of all men,* [3] *show which one of these two thou hast chosen to take the place in this ministry and apostleship from which Judas turned aside.*"

The Petition

Now, finally, we may make a clear statement of the reason for our prayer, the supplication. It is no longer the blurt-begging of a self-centered people, more conscious of their needs than of their Deity. It is rather the obedience of a faithful people whose very plea is shaped by the will of their dear Lord.

Absolutely any request, approached in this form of praying, may be set before God, no matter how outrageous or how minor it seems. It is the nature of God to cover the entire scope of human affairs.

Angry? Are you angry? Speak it to God. Are you angry even *at* God? Yes, so was the prophet Jeremiah, and

Jeremiah spoke it directly to the Lord—and because prayer is conversation, the Lord spoke back unto him. There is no better place for your rage to be stated than before a God who will not shy from you nor punish you but will change you as you have need.

Are you appointed to pray before a large group of people? Can you perceive their need? Then build your prayer around that petition, and state the petition here, in the center of it.

Everything from the passionate to the formal, from supplications most private to the grand and public orison—this central sentence of the five parts of the collect can bear it.

The Purpose

But even yet the prayer is not complete. A naked statement of need now must be woven both into the good designs of our God and into the community of Christians at large. "So that," we now say. Grant this thing, Lord, *so that* such and such a blessing may come of it. Here, O Lord, is how we shall use your goodness for a broader benefit than our own.

In this part anything selfish is washed away. In this fourth part of the collect even our private dramas (though no one else need know of this) are shared spiritually with all the people of God. In this part the good *ends* of our immediate requests are considered, so that we do not stop with ourselves, but reach beyond this thing and this moment into a blessed future and service to God.

"O Creator and Sustainer of the universe," prays the farmer, "unto whom all creatures look for their food in due season, please send rain upon our dry crops, *so that* the bounty which we reap shall be a sign of your merciful kindness and of our stewardship, a food for the health of many people. . . ."

Or, more beautifully stated in a prayer from the 1600s:

1. *Almighty God,*
2. *who hast blessed the earth that it should be fruitful and bring forth abundantly whatsoever is needful for the life of humankind:*
3. *Prosper, we beseech thee, the labors of the farmer, and grant such seasonable weather*
4. *that we may gather in the fruits of the earth ever rejoicing in thy goodness, to the praise of your holy name.*

The fourth part looks outward again. It places those who pray under the guidance of God once again. It acknowledges the true webbing, the interconnections, of the Church and of all creation. It devotes every gift of God (every petition which the Lord chooses to grant us) back into his kingdom and his service.

Here, now, is the wonderful balance of the collect. Just as the second part remembered the promises of God to us, this part makes promises of our own back to God. Just as the second part was a confession of our faith in God's actions, this is a pledge of personal commitment, that *our* actions shall serve God in return.

The Ending

Return again, just before *amen*, to a pure contemplation of God alone, revealed in his Son Jesus Christ.

Almost all the collects end with the words: "through Jesus Christ, your Son, our Lord." The repetition should never deaden our ears to the miracle embraced by them;

rather, repeating these words at the end of every prayer should draw such meditation that we marvel more and more at the kindness of a God who has granted us the opportunity and the right to pray!

We say *through Jesus Christ, your Son, our Lord,* because our whole prayer stands firmly on Jesus' loving generosity. He said, "Truly, truly, I say to you, if you ask anything of the Father, he will give it to you *in my name.* Hitherto you have asked nothing *in my name;* ask, and you will receive, that your joy may be full" (John 16:23–24). Not only does Jesus give us the invitation, but he himself makes a way for such praying: he it is who blew open the door between us and the transcendent Deity.

"First of all," Paul writes Timothy, "I urge that supplications, prayers, intercessions and thanksgivings be made for all people, for kings and all who are in high positions, that we may lead a quiet and peaceable life, godly and respectful in every way. This [such rich praying] is good, and it is acceptable in the sight of God our Savior, who desires all to be saved and to come to the knowledge of the truth." So these are the public consequences of praying: peace in our daily lives; in our behavior, holiness before God and respect toward others; salvation for more and more people upon the face of the earth, and the spreading of the knowledge of God's truth. Paul lists some of the most important *So that's*—purposes—for all our petitions.

And then he announces the power that fulfills them, the way between ourselves and our God, the foundation of all our praying:

"For there is one God, and there is one mediator between God and men, the man Christ Jesus." He *is* the Way. He draws God and us together. And how was this miracle accomplished in the first place? He "gave himself as a ransom for all"(1 Timothy 2:1–6).

So at the core of our praying is the cross, Christ and his holy sacrifice. He *is* the door through which we meet the Father.

Therefore the fifth part of the collect places all that we've prayed under the name of Jesus:

Through Jesus Christ, your Son, our Lord. Amen.

And so done is well done, indeed. We began wholly focused on our God; we end focused on our mediator to God.

The very form of this prayer has led us in utter sentiments higher than we might have been capable of on our own. This is what it means to pray with the whole Christian Church on earth, even if not another human soul is near to hear what we are saying.

7

PRAYING WITH JESUS, WHOSE WORD IS DEED

Jesus "was praying in a certain place, and when he ceased one of his disciples said to him, 'Lord, teach us to pray, as John taught his disciples.' And he said to them, 'When you pray, say: *Father* . . .'" (Luke 11:1–2).

So the disciples learned from the Lord's own mouth the several petitions of that prayer which we still call "The Lord's." And we still pray it. Believers all around the globe pray the elegant, elemental, comprehensive, bold and humble prayer—mostly in the words preserved in Matthew 6:9–13.

As we prayed with the psalmist, and with the faithful of the Church, so we may pray with Jesus. He gave us these words to make our own.

But he also gave us the remarkable insight that words of prayer may match prayerful deeds, until we have begun to live *a life of prayer!* It is this which is mostly missed about his teaching. He taught his disciples the same prayer at two times and in two ways; for he who said, "Pray, *Our Father who art in heaven . . . thy will be done,*" then went forth and actually performed his prayer, did it, enacted it, accomplished the same thing in his body and soul.

After the Master had taught the lesson of prayer, he went out and *became* the lesson.

It is night. A cold light falls from the stars; dim patches of pale light run over the heads of shoulders of four men walking among the trees of a garden.

Listen! One man is groaning aloud.

This one now separates himself and moves yet deeper into the trees, while the other three wait, then sit, then nod, then sleep.

The groaning man is totally alone. For a moment he stands swaying, as if he were dizzy. Suddenly he crumples down to the ground.

"Abba!" he cries. *"Abba!"*

The sound is strangled in his throat. His lips, so close to dry ground, spit dust in the darkness. His fingers clutch soil in desperation, and he prays:

"Abba, Father! All things are possible to thee!"

⟨∞⟩

Do you recognize the scene? Of course. It is Jesus' agony in the Garden before the soldiers come to arrest him. But keep closely in your mind that prayer which he taught the disciples, and watch how he elevates prayer from a matter of the mind and tongue to a mode of holy being.

Jesus' life and death declare that it isn't words alone that make up a prayer. It is deeds and passion and experience—the whole person, dramatically involved. Words alone can be as hollow and irrelevant as Ping-Pong balls.

And in praying do not heap up empty phrases as the Gentiles do; for they think that they will be heard for their many words. Do not be like them, for your Father knows what you need before you ask him. Pray then

87

like this: *Our Father who art in heaven, hallowed be thy name. Thy kingdom come, thy will be done, on earth as it is in heaven. Give us this day our daily bread; and forgive us our debts, as we also have forgiven our debtors; and lead us not into temptation, but deliver us from evil.*

Those are the words.

Now watch the garden scene unfold and see that prayer itself can be the expression of an event in progress. It is faithful and obedient action. It is human experience finding its voice—and by that voice directing itself wholly (action, emotion, thought, spirit, trust and love) toward God.

Behold how the Lord's prayer actually *happens*.

☙

—Jesus cries out (as may we all) his true and desperate desire "that, if it were possible, the hour might pass from him." This is the living substance of the sixth petition of the spoken prayer: *Lead us not into temptation*—the temptations of those who love neither God nor us. Another right rendition of that petition is, "Save us from the time of trial," of horrible testing, of "temptation."

Though his prayer is intensely personal and private, yet by his action he embraces his disciples in the same petition, for he says with sympathy and sorrow to the sleeping three what he said in the prayer: "Watch and pray that you may not enter into temptation."

—Over and over again—three times, deeply—the Lord Jesus begs the Father to "remove this cup from me." The cup of suffering; the cup of the sin of the whole of history; the cup of death. *Deliver me, deliver me, deliver me from evil*—the seventh petition is agonized so terribly that he sweats, as it were, great drops of blood.

—And over all, this supplicant casts an attitude of faithful obedience, while under all the Savior offers himself in perfect humility, himself becoming the third petition of the prayer. "Yet not what I will," he whispers, "but what thou wilt."

In this circumstance, how complete (and how sacrificial) is his submission to the will of God. Jesus is prepared for *any* answer—as the words of the Lord's Prayer should prepare us for any answer God may choose to give any other petition: *Thy will be done, on earth as it is in heaven.*

And because Christ, the most obedient petitioner of all, did more than mouth this petition; because he truly bowed his heart before the Father's will, despite the indescribable horrors it cost him, we are saved. The Lord's (enacted) Prayer is the beginning of salvation in the world. Jesus not only prayed to teach us prayer; he became his prayer in order to become *our* prayer, the right and the power of our praying.

—But implicit in the fact that he entered "the hour" of trial after all, implicit in his ultimate devotion to the will of God, is this: Jesus believed that "the time was fulfilled. The kingdom of God was at hand." By his praying, and then by his obeying the answer which God gave his prayer *(No, but you shall drink the cup)*, the kingdom of heaven is ushered into the world. In this manner, the second petition of the Lord's word-prayer is fulfilled in his deed-prayer: *Thy kingdom come.*

—Jesus began the teaching prayer, *Our Father*. So also he begins the prayer which consumes his whole being, "Abba. Papa. Daddy."

Does the invocation *Our Father* sometimes seem a formal invocation, a cool signal sent unto heaven that a certain communication is about to follow? Not any more! Now it's a plea. Now it's a child crying out of extreme need: "Now! Here! Me! You! Please! Do! Save me!" Urgency and the basic relationship are in the title and the cry.

These begging words arise from the immediate experience.

And then they themselves begin to constitute the experience, since they are the yelps of naked need. Moreover, they plead a further experience, the response of God in intimate love to the petitioner. Jesus cries, "*Abba,* Father," not only to teach us how to pray, but also to point us toward the source of our being, and then to introduce us to that source by his dependence on his "Papa," by holy obedience and death and resurrection.

In his extremity—by his extremity—he reveals that the transcendent Deity is also very intimate unto us, the parent apart from whom we cannot survive; and we say the same when we say, "Father, *our* Father."

⁂

"*Abba,*" groans the solitary man in the garden, "remove this cup from me." Then he holds his breath, awaiting the answer. He truly means his prayer. That he prays the prayer three times does not signify vain repetition; it signifies an absolute and complete sincerity.

"Nevertheless," he whispers, because he is faithful, "not what I want ... what you want ... do."

The answer comes. The answer is in God's perfect silence. It is this cosmic silence that turns Christ's word back upon himself: *Do.*

And so he rose up and woke his disciples and *did.*

Christ's whole life reflected his verbal dialogue with the Father. He did not, therefore, teach us mere recitation. He called us into the same dialogic relationship with his Father, and then he solemnized the relationship on the cross.

Go thou and *do* likewise.

For the veracity of what you say in prayer shall be revealed in how you live the prayer—and then your living and doing shall become a ceaseless praying unto the intimate God, our Father.

—How, then, shall we pray the fifth petition, *Forgive us our debts as we forgive our debtors?* Do you see now why the asking and the acting are here so completely connected that they cannot be separated without violating the true praying of the Lord's Prayer?

Amen, indeed.

8

OH, HOW RADIANT IS SHE WHO PRAYS!

*T*hanne and I worship regularly in the vast Chapel of the Resurrection on the campus of Valparaiso University. It seats several thousand in an airy space so filled with light and lightness and height, that the worshipers look like a low, plowed field under the vaults of heaven. There is a stark simplicity to the soaring clear windows and the walls of the nave.

The Chapel's greater ornament is in the chancel. There, three stained-glass windows swoop up to the fluted roof of a lofty silo of light. Ministers are diminished. Beneath the roof, as tall as a tree and standing free, is a cross from which a shining figure seems to be throwing himself forward in victory. His arms are lifted impossibly high. He is not crucified. He is triumphant.

Such bright glory can take away the breath of one who worships and prays in that place.

Not Thanne's. Not her breath. Her breath is reserved for an exercise more dear and difficult.

On Sundays we ascend stone steps into that towering chancel of glass, Thanne and I. We kneel around the victorious cross and a marble altar as wide as my dining room. We take bread and wine into ourselves, a tiny meal of eternal nourishment. Christ comes and touches us.

Then we rise and descend again into the endless nave, where Thanne finds her pew and sits and shrinks deeply into herself.

My wife bows her head, as private as a ladybird—and prays.

It doesn't matter how grand the room is: Thanne is in a small place, praying.

While the congregation continues to ascend and descend the chancel steps, while I sit singing three full hymns and all their verses, this woman does not cease to pray, humble and holy under glory.

Thanne, what are you praying for?

I am praying for my children.

She doesn't weep like Hannah, though she may have reason. She doesn't cry out like Jairus or beg like the Syrophoenician woman. She approaches God silently, with confidence and decorum.

And with love.

She is the priest who loves both God and her children, who speaks profoundly for each to the other.

Thanne, who are you praying for?

I know the answer. She is praying for our youngest daughter, Talitha. She is thanking God for bringing the child safe this far, and begging God to follow the woman into her future.

Our adopted daughter graduated from Spelman College this month. Everyone was there to honor her. *Everyone.* Not only Thanne and I but also her birth parents, Mary and Carter, and her birth grandmother, Trula. This was the first time we had met the Black side of Talitha's blood, and the meeting was genuinely blessed. Trula told us that she had prayed for the grandbaby always, and especially on her birthday. So Thanne had had a silent partner.

So God had hovered over the child in goodness even unto her graduation. And now that same child is backpacking alone through Mexico. Therefore, Thanne continues to pray—

My wife keeps her eyes closed, her face lowered in repose. I smell wine on her breath. Hundreds of voices, like sea-waves in the cavernous chapel, are singing: "Let us praise God together on our knees," while Thanne prays for her children.

I know the sounds inside her soul. I have heard the shape her praying takes.

She's praying for her other daughter, Mary, whom she hasn't seen for a year, whom she won't see another year yet. After *she* graduated spring of '95, Mary left the continent altogether. She felt a holy call to teach missionary children. She applied for a position in Cameroon, West Africa—and the laughing, faithful, healthy woman was chosen. She left O'Hare last August, while her mother waved and her father wept. Since then Mary has suffered one hellacious case of malaria; she has had to defend herself against the tough attacks of certain superiors—but she is well again and in love with her students—and here, in America on a Sunday morning in the drenching light of the Chapel of the Resurrection, her mother is lifting her name up to God.

Thanne's children are flowing away like streams down the sides of a beautiful mountain. But they have never left the tender springs beneath her heart.

Thanne? Who are you praying for?

Matthew. For my son Matthew.

Ah, yes: Matthew. And what do you pray for him?

That he be free of the demons of this society. That he rise in the certainty of his own endowments. That he rest in the certainty of God's undying love. That he take the hand of his truer parent and never, never let it go.

We are Matthew's adoptive parents.

The Truer One to whom Thanne refers—that is God. And in this moment she is, yes, Hannah: *I lend him to the Lord. As long as he lives, Matthew is lent to the Lord.*

At the wide altar the presiding ministers (small before the high Niagara of stained glass) are moving toward the completion of their service and the sacrament.

My wife might as well be sitting in St. Antony's cave.

She is praying for her firstborn, Joseph, a man so tender in spirit that the world around him is both exquisite and funny and dangerous. And she is naming other names besides his. She's praying for those to take our place in his future. Almost I hear her whisper the name of a woman, a dear woman, the one who shall increase as we decrease.

They all flow from her now, all the children. But prayer keeps the contact. By prayer she remains their silent, private priest. She is the burning one who bears them up and down the ladder of earth and heaven.

Who are you praying for, Thanne?

For you.

I can scarcely stand it! She is praying for me.

Once, early in our marriage, Thanne asked that we pray aloud together. I hesitated. Today I confess that the idea caused me discomfort—something a bit too intimate to be done in front of another human, even one's spouse. I was attending the seminary, preparing for ministry; but I liked things more formal, less personal. I hesitated, then, for weeks and months.

But there came the day wherein I committed some sin against Thanne. When I tried to make it right again between us ("Thanne, what can I do to prove my love for you?") she said, "We have to pray aloud together. We have to."

Guilt was greater than bashfulness. I agreed.

So after our tiny son Joseph was asleep, we went into our bedroom. I turned out the light. We lay fully dressed in darkness on the bedspread and in silence for a while.

I said, "I'll start."

Of course I would start. I was studying for the ministry. I was the husband. It was my duty. Besides, I was a wizard at words.

So I prayed in heavy cadences, like a hymnal, grandiloquent and measured and gassy with abstractions. When I was done I congratulated myself on having accomplished the difficult thing after all.

But then the voice of my wife arose in the darkness. In simple language, she was talking to God. Just talking. And her tone was so soft, it seemed that they were alone together, while I was allowed to listen, like an eavesdropper.

Her humility humbled me. There was no grandeur left in my soul.

And then, as she was speaking to God, she named my name! Not to me, but to God she murmured "Wally" with such love and gentleness that I began to cry. In the plain precincts of her prayer Thanne's love became a holy thing. It brought the breathing Spirit of God down upon my silly soul, and I cried.

Her praying was immediately God's answering.

What room may be furnished more beautifully than the heart where prayer is? For in that room God is.

Now, in the magnificent Chapel of the Resurrection the congregation stands up to sing the post-Communion canticle, and human voices ride the thunder of a mighty organ.

Thanne, too, stands. No one looks at her. Of course not.

None can see the miracle but me—that there are six of us standing together and that the one in the center, being filled with the Spirit of God, burns like the seraphim.

For this, too, is the thing that faithful praying accomplishes: it gathers in spirit those that have scattered far and far away.

Look, Thanne! Your sons shall come from afar, your daughters borne in arms—and you shall see and be radiant.

TWO
GOD LISTENS

᰾᰾᰾

9

THINE IS THE POWER

A child is sick. It is the middle of the night, and she has only half awoken in a sweaty fever. Fantastic images swoop and gibber in her bedroom. She begins to rock her head left and right, and softly the child moans.

Pay attention to her moaning. It forms no words, no articulate communication. Yet the whole of her distress drives the note of her moaning through a sliding scale higher and higher.

She's trembling. The hair sticks to her forehead.

She says, "Ma—" Not yet a whole word.

It doesn't matter. Immediately upon the sounding of that syllable, the hall light glows, and the bedroom door opens ushering gentle light into the baby's darkness, scattering the furies of her dreaming, granting the child a kind and solid presence for her eyes to see: for framed in the light of the doorway is the beautiful shape of her mother.

Swiftly, then, the woman enters, strokes the flesh of her baby, leaves and returns with cool moist cloths, with a little cracker and much juice and healing hands and companionship the whole night through.

So, then: a full communication was accomplished between the baby's waking and her sleeping again.

Who initiated it? Why, the child.

But who empowered it? Not the child. She was sick and groaning, that's all. She scarcely knew her trouble;

she couldn't put words to the noise she made; the noise was neither a question nor a calling; it was diffuse and undirected, the spontaneous response to hurting.

Nevertheless, it was heard by another! More than that, it was interpreted, which is what *listening* is. And immediately with understanding came the active response of a mother whose love is nearly omniscient, whose heart is almost omnipresent.

So who shaped a cry into communication? Who gave it direction and power, that it might be dialogue after all? Of course: the baby's mother.

It is the same between us and our God.

However inarticulate, however ignorant or misdirected our prayer may be, however weak in every respect (weak, mind you, *even in our ability to believe that it will be heard!*) it is the listening of the Lord God which makes our mumble a prayer.

Too often we have heard it said that if one prays without believing, one's prayer cannot be answered. This places the weight of *right* praying upon the poor, sick child. It therefore blames the child if it seems a prayer was not answered. And it assumes that the power of prayer lies here, with her—not there, with her God.

But God will be God, even in the exchange of common praying.

So let us say, little child, that your trust is waning. You suffer one sort of dis-ease or another, and it seems to you that the Lord has forgotten you. In fact, you say so.

You say, "The Lord has forsaken me."

It is as if you heaved a great groaning in the night, undirected, the plain utterance of spiritual pain.

But straightway, the light goes on in the hallway! Whether you see it or not, whether you hear it or not,

God listens. God comes and attends you. God does this thing!

Open the door and see. Isaiah 49:14 and the subsequent verses are the listening response of the Lord:

"Can a woman forget her sucking child, that she should have no compassion on the son of her womb? 'Even these may forget, yet I will not forget you.'"

God is like that mother whose ears are great dishes of listening. You cannot sigh, but that your Creator hears it! And the "compassion" that God feels for you is the same that a loving mother experiences deeply, deeply for the child of her womb: the Hebrew word for "compassion" derives from *raham*, which means "womb." It is in this place of generation and profound loving that the Lord God remembers you.

What you utter God hears. What God hears becomes, through grace and compassion, a prayer.

"Behold, I have graven you on the palms of my hands."

This is how intimate you are with your Creator: where God is, there you are. You are tattooed onto the hands that hold the world. And then, a second time, you are tattooed by the points of nails into the hands of Jesus, who died in order to open the door between you and his Father.

⌒⌒⌒

But God's listening is even more searching than that of a loving mother. His listening needn't wait for the groan at all. His listening, in fact, is the very context of all prayer. It *precedes* our praying, so that we pray into a divine and merciful awareness already waiting, already knowing the thing we are about to say.

"Thou searchest out my path and my lying down," says the psalmist, "and art acquainted with all my ways.

Even before a word is on my tongue, lo, O LORD, thou know-est it altogether" (Psalm 139:3–4).

Jesus affirms this same watchful omniscience of the Father in his Sermon on the Mount: "Your Father knows what you need before you ask him" (Matthew 6:8).

His knowing is the authenticity, the force, the joy, the goodness and the reality of our communication.

What then? Should we therefore turn the whole business over to God? If he can read minds, why not give our full attention to the affairs of this world and let him do the searching, the listening and the answering all on his own. He doesn't need our first word, does he?

Ah, but there is a difference between *need* and *want,* even with God.

When she was still a round toddler on short legs, I had sharp eyes for my daughter Mary. Love turned sight into insight. If she bent her head and stared at her right shoe; if she began to take odd steps, heaving that shoe higher and higher, only to stomp it harder down; if perplexity filled her blue eyes—even before she lifted her face to find me, I *knew* the word forming itself on her tongue. *"Can you,"* she was going to say, *"Daddy, can you tie my shoe?"*

Now, I could go to the tender child yet before the word was spoken and tie the shoe. I didn't need the word, did I?

But I wanted it. I delighted in it.

I would wait for those dear blue eyes to find mine, wait for the chunky child to stump toward me and perhaps crawl into my lap and touch my face and say out loud, "Daddy? Tie my shoes?"

Because it's the relationship which causes me such pleasure. I love her. I love her love in return. How could I miss the moment which makes us an *Us* together?

Moreover, if I merely reached down to help her without these expressions of love and trust, she might assume my help a mechanism of the universe, the cold duty of daddies. How much richer and truer is my help when it clearly comes of my love?

And so with God: it's not just the service of the Deity unto humankind, but the relationship that matters. Love and trust are the supreme purposes of prayer: that we pray in a loving trust to our dear Father, and that he answers out of his infinite store of merciful love.

Ask, therefore. Though God's is surely the power, yet "the Lord waits to be gracious to you" (Isaiah 30:18). Ask first, and what you receive you'll know to have come of graciousness, and you will glorify no one but your Father who is in heaven.

THREE

GOD SPEAKS

〜〜〜〜

INTRODUCTION

It is God's nature to speak. The first event of the universe was a brief, spectacular utterance: *"Let . . ."* The first word God ever spoke answered no human prayer, nor responded to anything outside of the Divine Self, for there was not yet anything but that Self in serene sufficiency. Rather, that first word gave voice to his own holy yearning. *Let there be . . . .*

And once God had spoken the thing, his speaking *was* the thing: *Light!*

O children of God, consider what kind of speaking your Father can do! His word is more than a murmured, parental consent. It is more than condemnation or argument or denial, more than commanding or compelling or referring. You do not rush to dictionaries in order to discover the meanings of his words. The meanings are self-evident. His words are their own meanings, as light is light—and light is *seen*, light is *experienced* by our mortal flesh and senses; light cannot be tucked into the pages of a book of abstract definitions, as if human words could now define the creations of the Creator. Look! God's word can cause to be what had not been before. His words bulk as indisputable realities in the cosmos.

Do you understand the implications? If your Father speaks you—not *to* you, but if he utters *you* as the subject of his pronunciation—why, then *you are*.

It is God's nature to speak. The second sort of word he spoke at creation was the naming word: *And God called the light Day.* From that point on God did not cease to name the things that were. But the words which were

109

names did not merely point to things the way signs point to the things they can only represent ("Chicago, 300 miles"). No, when God names something or someone, that name declares its relationship with everything else, and with everyone else, and with God himself. So "Day" is related to "Night," and "the Heavens" are related to "the Earth" exactly as "Earth" relates to the "Seas."

God took the man named "Jacob," the *grabber*, the *usurper*, the one whose nature it was to trip up others, and named that man "Israel": *He Strives with God*. Here is a pun, for this one, who has striven against God, now by the grace of God becomes a prince, striving on the side of God. The name declares the new nature of the man precisely because the name declares a new relationship between this man and God—and between this man and all other people thereafter, starting with his brother Esau, before whom the new Israel soon bows in perfect humility.

Do you, children of God, understand the implications? When Jesus says of you, "The sheep hear his voice, and he calls his own sheep by name and leads them out" (John 10:3), that divine "name-calling" declares your relationship with the Father. God's Son—the Shepherd who has made you his sheep and who has called you by your personal name—has thereby declared you to be a child of the Heavenly Father. When the God who spoke you into existence next speaks your name, why, *you are his!*

It is God's nature to speak. His first word created. His second word named. His third word delights in the things he has made and named: "And God saw everything that he had made, and behold, it was very *good*." The Hebrew word for "good" implies more than a mere assessment of the worth of creation, "Yes, it meets the standards." It suggests that God's third word is filled with feeling, pleasure, joy, glee, a perfect gratification: it is exactly what God had hoped it would be! Yes! *Yes!*

Moreover, this sort of word, *very good,* allows for the more complex reactions that one may have to a thing of nearly unspeakable beauty (speakable, perhaps, only by the Deity, the source of beauty). How beautiful are the mountains? And how do we respond to them? How beautiful the child of bright innocence? They are good. Good!

What is this "good," this responding, assessing, delighting third word of the speaking God? Why it is his own character, reflected in his creations: "O give thanks to the Lord, for *he is good,* for his steadfast love endures forever." And there, like a shining water, is the source of goodness: the love of the Lord.

And can you now see implications even before I present them? If the God who spoke you into existence, the God who named you his child, also speaks your name in the same delight that he speaks the goodness (the *very* goodness) of creation; if the tone of his utterance is one of endless affection, why, then *you are beloved.*

You are.

And you are his.

And you are his beloved child.

That is the quality of God's conversation even yet today after he has listened to your speaking and then takes his turn to talk. No matter what the Lord says specifically, this is the frame and the relationship in which he says it: a dear Father speaking unto his dear child.

Do you sometimes doubt this blessed, parental nature of God's listening and speaking? Are you sometimes filled with the forboding that he will refuse to speak?—that he is a God of Absence, Abandonment and Silence? Or do you fear that he will answer in anger?

I understand. I, too, have experienced an aggrieved separation from the God of Righteousness. I, too, have heard his fourth sort of word.

It is in the nature of God to speak—not just to make and to name and to declare relationship, but also to announce the breaking of relationship: sin. God will not only say "Good" of that which delights him, but also "Not Good" of that which denies him:

> See, I have set before you this day life and good, death and evil. If you obey the commandments of the LORD your God ... the LORD your God will bless you in the land .... But if your heart turns away and you will not hear ... I declare to you this day that you shall perish, ... I call heaven and earth to witness against you this day, that I have set before you life and death, blessing and curse; therefore choose life. (Deuteronomy 30:15–19)

But I have often chosen to turn away. I have chosen myself over God. I have not chosen *good* but, rather, *evil*. Therefore, where God desires my life, I chose my death. Under such a circumstance, relationship is sundered, and between me and God there falls such a gulf that I am one abandoned, suffering the silence and the absence of God only. There would, in the separation of death, be no hearing when I spoke, nor any speaking that I myself would want to hear.

But there is a fifth sort of word from our merciful (*good!*) God. It is as powerful as the first, for it re-creates. It is as covenental as the second, for it joins what had been broken, it marries what had been divorced, it brings to life what has been dead, it names new names, and thereby establishes new relationships forever. This fifth word is more lovely than the third, for it springs from the highest mercy of the Heavenly Father, and the deepest love—

to love when those he loves are enemies and sinners and most unlovely. And this fifth word overcomes utterly the fourth word of wrath.

God's most potent, most revealing, most beautiful Word of all is: *Jesus*—the Word which was from the beginning after all, existing even before God uttered the universe; the Word which still today is light and life; the Word which is the Self of God come near to us, the Word which became flesh and dwelt among us, full of grace and truth.

It is in the nature of God to speak. The entire life of Christ, then, from incarnation to death to resurrection and ascension, is the re-echoing shout of the Father: *I love you! You are mine. When you pray to me, I will listen. And having heard you, I will answer. I will never cease to heed you nor to speak to you—for it is my nature to speak.*

☙⚬❧

In what follows I will touch upon some of the various means by which God speaks to us. Surely, I cannot present them all; but perhaps my few will prompt you to become alert to the many, many voices of God.

The Scriptures are a host of languages: song, story, exhortation, law, wisdom, thoughtful theology—and the Good News itself, the Gospel of Jesus. Through Scripture continually the Holy Spirit brings us to the knowledge of the truth, granting us sudden insights and warm passions as answers to our very explicit praying. Surely, then, the Christian will daily return to this living, murmuring letter from the Father, listening ever with new ears to hear new words—or else to hear the old words repeated with new force and purpose.

Moreover, the Christian who thinks that she has heard the voice of God elsewhere will always return to the

Bible in order to confirm what she has heard. If she can find that God has spoken this same way in the past, recorded in the Bible, then she may assure herself that, yet, it was God she heard this day too. In other words, the Bible is not only the present dialogue of God, it is also a kind of grammar-book of *how* God talks. Have you heard God in the voice of a child, in something a child did or said? Check to be sure. Go to the Bible in order to see whether God has spoken through the mouths of babes and sucklings before. Yes? He has? And what meanings does such speaking have? How does it work?

The Bible is the dictionary of the God whose nature it is to speak. Even when you are not looking up specific references, learn it thoroughly, so that your ears will be *always* attuned to the voice of God in creation, in people, in events, in your experience—yes, and in *your* behavior and in your own soul.

I HEARD THE SAVIOR CALL MY NAME

On the northeastern shores of Lake Michigan, about 120 miles south of the Straits of Mackinac, the lake bed rises to form a long ridge close beneath the surface of the water. Some 200 yards offshore that ridge lightens the still water into a long green smile. If one climbs the high bluffs back of the beach, one can on a calm day recognize the submerged formation as if it were the scaled, stony back of a sleeping sea-snake.

But on windy days it is the white breaker that reveals where the stone lies below: it foams far offshore, it combs the bearded face of the lake and stands on one foot, then crashes down with the sound of enormous weight. Such heavings of the sea have swamped more than one sailing ship. I saw the wreckage of a nineteenth-century schooner still lying in six feet of water. It was called *The Hiawatha*.

In the 200 yards between the offshore shallows and the beach itself, the seabed sinks again, and the lake deepens to twenty or thirty feet—too deep, at any rate, for me to dive down and touch the bottom.

I spent the summer of my seventeenth year working as a lifeguard several miles north of this more treacherous reach of water. But I knew the spot.

It was my duty, too, to conduct daylong hikes through the denser woods inland, emerging in sunlight at the very top of the bluff that overlooked that underwater ridge-formation. A wonderful path of pure sand descended from the top to the bottom of the bluff. Imagining myself Moses, I would stand at the head of the path and send my hikers downhill, warning them neither to run nor to enter the water (never, in fact, to swim anywhere but in the designated areas where I could see to save them). In those long-ago days I was rejoicing in my own emerging freedom. I had a girlfriend of dark, enduring beauty, Barbara, who walked with me on these hikes, whose presence elevated my sense of personal importance and grandeur. When, therefore, the hikers whom I had led had all gone down, when they were safe and small on the beaches below, I would raise my Moses staff and sweep it toward the north, their last injunction from me, their final direction home.

Now, I will confess that twice (but both times in the company of the dark Barbara; I was not alone; neither was I without terrible temptations, since Barbara seemed to me as beautiful as Miriam when she danced with her timbrel above the bloody sea!)—twice, I say, when all my hikers had vanished toward the north, I ran. I mean: I dropped like a heavenly bolt down the sandy path, I shot out across the beach, and I fairly flew into the waters of Lake Michigan, swimming mightily a hundred yards from shore, jolted by the sudden cold on my sweating body.

It was delightful. And it was then that I tried to touch the bottom, and failed. Too deep. Too deep for me.

෴

In this chapter we must begin with God's first, his broadest, his most fundamental response to all our speaking. It undergirds every particular word he may choose to say. It gives context to every individual topic he may utter. And it assures us that some answer will always be given to every prayer we pray.

God's profoundest word to us is this: LIFE. It is his desire that no one should perish but that all his children should live. He calls us from dying to living. The essence and the power of his every answer is this gift of life. Whenever God talks, those whom he addresses—those who hear him—are vibrantly alive in the relationship itself, whatever the immediate issue. Before we consider the various ways by which the dear Lord speaks to his children, we must first grow alert to the divine desire which motivates him always, always to communicate with us. At the same time, we must become wisely aware of the various ways we would subvert God's desire by choosing death instead of life.

It is in the difference between these choices—life in the Lord, or an isolating death—that we will recognize what prayer is at the nexus: why God invites our speaking at all, why God answers, and what God hopes to be the consequence of every whispered petition, whether heavy or light.

⁓

If we resist the laws of God, we resist God. Without God, we create for our habitation a universe whose meaning must arise from our *selves* (our understanding, our personal value, our successes and accomplishments, our innate goodness, our hedonistic pleasures) and if these selves cannot finally sustain meaning in the universe, if the self is too small, too weak, too failing to save us, then (without God) we are left with no meaning whatsoever. How hollow and empty the world! How helpless and lonely are we.

If we lose ourselves in the endless maze of chemical dependencies; if we let certain hatreds become our bread, feeding upon them day and night as if they gave purpose to our existence; if we allow ourselves to drown in self-pity and the perpetual blaming of others for our circumstances; if, in other words, we live in lies, sundering ourselves from reality and a true recognition of our real (needful) selves, then we shall have forsaken God's good creation. We shall live imprisoned in the deep darkness and the emptiness of deception.

We shall have chosen death instead of life and blessing.

And death must soon trouble us with a colder, more bitter truth. Loneliness, meaninglessness, helplessness, darkness, despair—dying—must horrify us.

And then the prayer we pray shall not be elaborate. Indeed, the more elemental our cry, the fewer the words!

Help me, O God!

The fundamental prayer of the Hebrews which we have carried into our liturgies as a single word—*Hosanna!*—means "Save us, we beg you!"

In the matters of life and death our whole being becomes the prayer. A yearning to live, reduced to a single spontaneous communication, begins the process. And then it ought to be with our whole beings that we listen for the third part of praying, God's response. As our speaking was simple and short, so shall his speaking be. He may say no more than a name.

Our names, you see, the word by which the Shepherd leads; by which he establishes relationships and grants people a personal value; by which ("Lazarus! Come forth!") Jesus has raised the dead.

Listen for the simplest, most essential word in the mouth of the God whose nature it is to speak.

Listen for your name. And so be raised to life again.

⌀⟋⟍⟍⟍⟋

I don't recall the immediate reason for my wandering away from the camp community alone. At one point that summer John Blackstone took Barbara Witzke to a secluded spot at night, then returned to boast of prowess and conquests. Perhaps I was moping.

In the warm dark of an overcast night, in the still of a windless night, I walked south along the beach a mile, two miles. I lost myself in the languid thoughts of melancholy youth. I sank down and sat in the sand, suffering an exquisite loneliness, the sweet sorrow of an artist abandoned. And then, on a whim, I stripped and waded into the water. The bluff behind me was swallowed up in darkness. Invisible. Nevertheless it seemed to push me forward. Sand turned stony beneath my feet. I dived seaward and swam.

How long did I swim? I don't know. Slow strokes, slow strokes, I took a grim pleasure in solitude. Lo, how I have *become* my world! Surely, Moses, abused by his own people, must have achieved an emotional self-sufficiency.

The surface water was warm, but currents from the deeps ran ribbons of chill across my skin. I could hear only the little waves lapping at my ears. I rolled left and right in a slow Australian crawl, and I swam.

Then nothing in particular happened. But suddenly I woke *to* the nothingness surrounding me and another sort of cold ran fingers into the core of my body. I stopped and sank and turned upright, treading water. I turned and turned, looking everywhere in blackness, seeing nothing, absolutely nothing!

There were no stars that night. No lights, no glow above the horizon—no horizon! No shore that I could see. And if the bluff was shadow in shadow, so was the air piled over the western extent of the lake only a heavier shadow. I could not distinguish one from the other.

The black was perfectly still. No wind, no waves, no slap of the waters. How could I decide directions without sound? The only break of water was the circle around my neck. I *was* my horizon. And my continent. Nothing near me to grab, nothing to stand on, nothing hard or stable or secure.

I was in a nowhere, and I began to panic. Everywhere was the same where. Which way should I swim? And how could I be sure that I was swimming in a straight line? Anywhere could be the wrong where and disastrous.

I tried to dive down to the bottom. No luck. Down and down, the dark grew cold. So I struck out and swam a certain direction, hard, for five minutes, and then I dived down again. Colder.

Out of the depths have I cried unto you, O LORD!

I sought to swim in the same direction again. Did I? I don't know. Turning and turning in a running world, I could not know. But I swam. And I dived again. And I touched the bottom.

It was stony, great smooth stones sunken in a sea-slime. I dived again and again and began to perceive an angle, a rising up. That, therefore, is the direction in which I swam. I swam with strong sweeps of my arms and a churning kick, almost as it were with my last energy, but with a tight anticipation: the beaches, and sand, and the land!

Then it occurred to me that I could, in fact, be swimming away from land, out toward the underwater formation which rose up 200 yards offshore!

And all at once my limbs began to tremble like rubber. Oh, I was so tired. I felt like crying. How did I know that I was not swimming out toward my death instead of home again?

O Lord, hear my voice.

I said, "Help." I swallowed water. I could not shout. I hung like a larva upon the surface of the sea, and I said, "Please help me."

Almost immediately a soft voice came out of the night uttering a single word as if it were a question: "Wally?"

I snapped alert. I turned in the water. Suddenly the world had focus and a direction.

"Wally, is that you?"

"Yes," I spluttered. "Yes, it's me!"

Well, it *was* me, and at that calling of my name I came to be again, yes. *Yes: I am! And I am here.*

"What are you doing out there?"

It was a woman's disembodied voice. It was Barbara Witzke ashore, calling me back from the sea.

No, but it was also my Savior calling me from death to life again. It was the third part of prayer, God's speaking in powerful language the word of his love, the word of my re-creation: *Wally,* he said, exactly as Jesus said *Mary* to his dear Magdalene the day of his resurrection, and hers.

෴

Even so does the Savior answer the desperate, spontaneous prayers of many who are perishing, whose universe has become dark, unstable, forsaken and empty.

Through the voices of those who love and forgive (Oh, the divinity in those acts!) God speaks. Professional counselors may be the speech of the healing Heavenly Father. Family members who are able to declare the truth in the face of self-deceptions; pastors, friends, neighbors, spouses, parents and children who can be a moral compass for the person who has literally lost his way—these are the instruments of God.

And they *are* the spoken communication of the Creator to the one who, dying, has cried out, "Help!" from the depths of his soul: "Please help me! *Hosanna!*"

"Yes," saith the Lord.

And then, in the voices of his angels, your helpers, he calls you by your name.

And that, still, is prayer.

11

SPEAKING THROUGH THE LESSER MESSENGERS

I must already now begin to speak about the fourth part of praying—our listening—even while I'm still discussing the third part, God's speaking. This is where our faith becomes important, for God will hear all prayers, whether by those who believe in him or by those who do not. And God will speak his reponse to every prayer. Every prayer!

But if we are not prepared to listen to God—to anything God might choose to say, for it is the Lord who is God, after all, and not we ourselves—then we will miss his speaking. And then it will seem to us that God didn't answer our prayer at all. But faith trusts enough to wait upon the speaking of the Lord. Faith believes that the God of creation will speak through his creation in a multitude of means.

Faith, moreover, is a way of being: it is being in such relationship with the Lord, that we become *willing* to pay a continual attention to him.

In the last chapter, those who begged God for help were prepared by their deep dread of dying to hear his response.

In this chapter—where we will consider how God calls us to account by his harsher words of judgment, often out of the mouths of babes and sucklings—our preparation must be a genuine humility!

Within the scope of our Christian faith is the piety of a life that tries to conform itself more and more to the desires of the dear Lord. By worship, by fasting and alms-giving and tithing, by regular Bible study and devout prayers, we Christians remember our right relationship unto God: that we must be humble before our Creator and our Redeemer.

If we are not meek in his presence, we may not hear accurately his communication to us. We may dismiss it as a false word, or we may dismiss his messengers as beneath our attention.

Listen: most often when God must utter judgment against our sinning, the voice he uses will be people considered less than ourselves, for they will have been the objects of our sinning. If we lack humility, we surely will lack regard for such messengers. Those who oppress others will scarcely give heed to the oppressed—*unless they truly believe in God (faith), believing that God loves the downtrodden, believing that God labors for righteousness and justice in the land.*

Do you see, then, that it is faith which hears God speak, especially when God chooses to say what we do not choose to hear?

∾

Once, grievously depressed, the prophet Jeremiah prayed an angry prayer straight to the Lord. He blamed God for the suffering and the sorrow he had to endure in life.

"Thy words were found, and I ate them," Jeremiah said. "I did not sit in the company of merrymakers, nor did I rejoice; I sat alone, because thy hand was upon me, for thou hadst filled me with indignation."

No parties for Jeremiah. Outrage, rather. Fierce solitude. And worse: "Why is my pain unceasing, my wound incurable, refusing to be healed?"

Then the prophet hurls at God an angry accusation: "Wilt thou be to me like a deceitful brook, like waters that fail?"

It's a figure of speech: he is blaming God for sending him away from any sustenance, as if the prophet had been sent into the desert with the promise that when he needed water, God would provide it. But, says Jeremiah, after going past the point of no return, nearly dying for thirst and turning aside to the waters that were promised, he finds them dried up! God is killing him!

That's the prayer. Jeremiah was surely right to pray his true feelings to God, even if they were wrong feelings after all.

And God answered the prayer! Of course: God will hear and answer every prayer. But the answer is a harsh word, a necessary word to curb the prophet's sinning.

And here is my point. Because Jeremiah was a faithful man, pious all his days and finally humble before God, he *could* hear and listen to responses which he would himself not have chosen.

Therefore thus says the LORD: *"If you return, I will restore you, and you shall stand before me. If you utter what is precious and not what is worthless, you shall be as my mouth"* (Jeremiah 15:15–19).

This is judgment. God seeks to change his prophet, to purify him by repentance. Though it is not the word Jeremiah thought he needed, it is an absolutely needful and loving word which seeks the atonement of a sinner.

So the God who by our name can lift us up to life again is the same God who by a hard word bends us down to see our sin and seek forgiveness.

I came home from church in a foul mood.

They pay their pastors to be good. So I am good. I'm good till it hurts. I grow weary with well-doing. I arbitrate among the several women's groups in the congregation. I console folks who have been insulted. I counsel couples who didn't come for counseling so much as they came each to get the pastor on his side, on her side, against the other.

On that particular day I'd spent time downtown arguing for the rights of those who live in the inner city. Exhausting. And there had been a morning funeral. Deep gloom and pitiful sadness for the grown children who had scarcely cared for their mother while she failed in her tiny apartment alone.

All excellent justifications for my foul mood, you see.

And when I got home for supper, when no one was paying me any more, I took a break from goodness.

Our children were little in those days. I suppose I shouldn't have blamed them for joyful noises. Incessant, high-pitched, every-room-in-the-house joyful noises. Let the four small furnaces explode all over the place.

But I had used up all my goodness.

So at suppertime I commanded them to sit in a perfect and godly silence. Two boys, seven and six; two girls, four and three—Joseph the oldest sat to my left, while Talitha the youngest sat to my right.

We prayed. "Come Lord Jesus, be our guest, and let these gifts to us be blessed. Amen."

It isn't as if I can actually remember praying that prayer. I probably gave it no more than a grain of thought. But we always prayed that prayer before we ate. We must have prayed it that night too.

And the Lord Jesus of holy righteousness did come, did speak, did almost utter his response into a vacuum of impious unpreparedness.

Midway through our peaceful meal, Talitha grew squirmy beside me.

I said, "Be quiet."

Perhaps she tried. But trying in her sounded like whining, and her body began to twist into the shapes of complaint and unhappiness.

"Talitha," I said, "I'm not in the mood. Be quiet."

She frowned. She stuck out a combative bottom lip. She picked up a piece of jelly bread between two fingers, rotated the morsel out over the floor.

"Don't," I said.

She looked hard at me and dropped the bread jelly-side down.

I moved my chair back, bent down and grabbed the bread. As I stood up, I made a small spring of my fore-finger and thumb, and I flicked the flesh on the back of Talitha's hand.

"I said, Don't," I said, then walked into the kitchen for a rag with which to wipe the floor.

When I came back the child was nearly swooning for sorrow. Talitha sobbed so deeply that her body shook. Water rained from her eyes. Her mouth smeared itself wide open.

"Oh, Talitha," I said, "that did not hurt you. It was just a little flick."

Now, after I had sat down and begun again to chew my food, Joseph, seven years old, tilted his chair back on my left side, tilted his head back too and stared up at the ceiling.

"Sometimes," he said, as if speaking to no one in particular, just thinking out loud: "sometimes Daddy spanks

127

us and we don't mind. We laugh. It's fun. Sometimes Daddy spanks us and we mind. On our birthdays he gives us a birthday spanking and a pinch to grow an inch. We like that. It doesn't hurt. But when he's angry it always hurts, no matter if it's just a little flick. It hurts."

Joseph rocked his chair forward and kept on eating. He never once looked at me.

He was just a kid! What does a kid know?

But my daughter's tears were tiny knives. And the guilt in me was real. Shame was my humility that day, shame my preparedness—and faith my ability to hear the hard word since I believed in the forgiving word to follow.

No, it wasn't just the kid.

It was the Lord Jesus himself who said to me, *If you return, I will restore you. If you utter what is precious and not what is worthless, Pastor, you shall be as my mouth again.*

12

SPEAKING THROUGH YOUR OWN IMPOSSIBLE DEEDS

*W*hen I was twelve years old," the woman said to me, "my father began to lie with me."

She used the biblical phrase *lie with* as if she were wearing a Victorian high-necked blouse and skirts to her ankles.

"We lived in a very big house," she said. "It was an old house. Big rooms, spacious rooms—but only a few rooms after all." She paused. "When I remember the feel of those days, all the sound is echoing. I was so little in such big rooms."

There is no reason for me to tell you this woman's name. We met several summers ago in the State of Washington where I was lecturing. She had an easy, disheveled manner—a most approachable person. Her hair and clothing were both clean and rumpled. So was her smile somewhat rumpled, as if smiling were the shape into which her face fell when her mind was busy elsewhere. When she listened intently, on the other hand, her smile grew fierce and she blinked rapidly.

In the pictures I have seen—daguerreotypes—Victorian women in high-necked blouses stand perfectly erect, their shoulders back, their chins up, their spines as straight as broomsticks.

The language of the woman took on such a propriety while she told me her story, but not her appearance. She seemed to strew herself when she sat, like an unfolded handkerchief.

"On the outside, our house was most handsomely large," she said.

We were facing one another over a table in the dining hall. Early afternoon. No one occupied the room but us. I sipped a cup of coffee.

"It was a thing of dignity," she said, "painted pure white, clean both cup and platter, pretty gingerbread carvings down the eaves and above the windows—like lacey eyelids. It looked closed. Our house looked reserved, private, so that one would have thought there was privacy within. But," the woman murmured, "the rooms were very big and very few. And I have five brothers. There was almost no privacy inside our house. Except that my mother saw nothing. My mother never saw anything."

I liked the woman before me. I had already noticed her during my lectures. She was not a note-taker; she was watchful, rather, a dramatic listener. Her expression was the immediate marriage of my word and her meditations.

One is inclined to perform a bit better for such rewarding attentions. I watched her in return and took pleasure in her bumptious face—until the morning of our conversation, when she grew more and more focused, like the flint of a slender arrow, aimed at me.

I had been discussing some of the "silent" women of the Old Testament—unto whom I hoped to give voice in a book I was working on then, a detailed retelling of the entire Bible narrative: *The Book of God*.

In chronological order, I was presenting three women: Leah, Jacob's first wife, who revealed her personal struggles and her grand survival in the names of her children; Jephtha's daughter, who suffered the consequences of her father's rash oath and died a sacrificial death; Tamar, King David's daughter, who was raped by his eldest son, who never received redress for the outrage, but who vanished from the biblical account with these words: *So Tamar dwelt, a desolate woman, in her brother Absalom's house.*

(Tamar's story is told in 2 Samuel 13. In order to understand the story of my own friend, I suggest you read it through.)

While Tamar stood wounded among us, the watchful woman raised her hand.

"Sleeves?" she said. "Little Tamar was beautiful, that's one thing. But you said she wore a long robe with sleeves?"

"Yes," I said.

"And sleeves, too, were beautiful?"

"Unusual. A mark of distinction," I said. "Joseph's 'coat of many colors' had long sleeves. But the biblical explanation regarding Tamar is that the virgin daughters of David wore long robes with sleeves."

My interrogator paused, staring at me and blinking rapidly. "A desolate woman?" she said.

"Yes. *De-solus.* One on her own. Abandoned."

"It's more than shame, you know," she said. She leaned forward, and then a series of thoughts shot forth like arrows from her forehead: "It's guilt. Her brother forced her and he lay with her, but Tamar's greatest desolation was that she believed it was her fault. Her own fault. Did the great King David, her father, ever even *talk* to her again? When everyone abandons you, it is your fault. So you abandon yourself as well. You crawl out of

131

your body and go away. That's the second greatest desolation. Now you are nothing in a nowhere."

Abruptly she sat backward. I expected a brazen expression then, as if daring me to blame her outburst— or else an expression of abject embarrassment. She showed neither.

She covered her mouth with the tips of three fingers and giggled. "Oops," she said, and raised her shoulders to her ears in a funny, perfectly peaceful apology.

Yes, I liked her very much.

I made a point to sit with her at lunch that day. It was raining, good reason to remain talking together as others left the dining hall. The woman was thirty-two, had never been married, but was just beginning to consider the notion with sincerity.

"It," she smiled, "seems a possible thing, now." She had small copper flecks in her irises. I felt a private pleasure in noticing them.

When we were alone, I said, "And what's the first greatest desolation?"

She glanced up. The woman knew immediately the source and the context of my question. This would alter radically our conversation, and she took a moment to assess my merit.

Then she tilted her head and answered. "The first greatest desolation is to believe that even God has abandoned you."

She waited. Now it was my turn to decide whether to pursue the topic and to suffer the story behind it.

I said, "Have you felt this?"

She said, "Yes. For four years. From the time I was twelve to the time I was sixteen."

"You were abandoned."

"I thought I was. And I prayed. All through those years I prayed to Jesus, *Love me, love me—Jesus come and help me. Amen. That was my prayer.*"

"Did Jesus answer it?"

"Yes. Always. But I didn't know that until just a few years ago."

"Why," I asked, "did you pray that prayer?" This was the question which, if she chose to answer it, would open the door.

The woman gazed at me a moment. Then she dropped her eyes to the cup on the table before her. Softly, with perfect articulation, she said, "When I was twelve years old, my father began to lie with me . . ."

As the clouds began to abandon the sky, this brave woman's story emerged in short strokes and bold sentences.

⚬⚬⚬

Countless are the mouths through which the dear Lord speaks to those who have spoken to him. Children may bear his word to us, even his harder word of judgment: *Repent, and believe in the Gospel.*

The friend who calls her friend by name may be uttering the resurrecting word of the Shepherd: *If God names you, then you are.*

Once in Alaska, God spoke by means of a mountain, and Thanne interpreted the meaning of his comforting word: *I am with you wherever you go.* Even so had God spoken to Israel by means of a pillar of cloud and a pillar of fire.

And to the frightened paperboy riding a Canadian bus, God sent an angel-messenger in the form of another paperboy who knew exactly where to go and what to do.

Countless, the means the Lord has for speaking—but one of the most exhilarating instruments for the voice of the presence of God *is yourself!*

He shall speak *to* you *through* you, if only you will take your own true measure. Know yourself first. Know and confess the genuine limits of your created being, for there are many things you can do, and some of those you do very well. But there are many more things which are far beyond your natural powers. You cannot come out of your body, not on this earth, not until you die; and the body that contains your life also confines it. There is neither shame nor blame in this: it is the natural limitation of creatures. Only the Creator can do all things. We, a little lower than the angels, are able to imagine marvelous things; but the imagination outreaches our abilities. We cannot *do* them. God alone can accomplish every single thing which he conceives. For God, to say it *is* to do it.

The primal sin and the source of sinning is our effort to be like God by taking upon ourselves this omnipotent authority: to do all we want to do, to become our own creators, to live as if we were our own gods. This is the Serpent's great lie, that we can break out of our creaturely limitations without dying. Dear people, as long as we sin this sin, God cannot speak within us—or at least we cannot hear him there, because we will continue to mistake his voice for our own! Every holy portion of our beings we will claim for ourselves.

Therefore I say: confess your limitations. That may first require of you a confession of the sin of self-deceit. If you have tried to be like God, if you have elevated yourself to stations you do not deserve, then you shall have lived in blindness a while, ignorant of the truth of your *self.*

Then, after the difficult self-examination of repentance and forgiveness, there follows very naturally self-knowledge: you are capable, you are lovely in the sight of God, but you are fundamentally different from God. Know your limits, the limits of flesh, even of the sentient flesh. Be at peace with these limits, seeing that the limitless God loves you and grants you in that relationship his own infinity.

Now you are prepared to recognize the miraculous voice of God within your own person! (And once again you see how it is *faith* that listens, faith that can recognize God's speaking back to us.)

For when you do *more* than you know you are able to do, that must be the true God working in you.

When you accomplish miracles, deeds you have neither the right nor the power to accomplish, that reveals the immediate presence of the Creator, whose natural action within creation must ever seem miraculous.

When Jesus sent seventy disciples to preach ("as lambs in the midst of wolves") he gave them "authority to tread upon serpents and scorpions, and over all the power of the enemy." They returned thereafter "with joy, saying, 'Lord, even the demons are subject to us *in your name!*'" (Luke 10:1–3, 17–19). It was clear to them that Jesus was the source of their miraculous deeds. What they accomplished transcended human capacities: "And he said to them, 'I saw Satan fall like lightning from heaven!'" What they accomplished, therefore, revealed the name and the power and the presence of Jesus within them.

It is the same with us.

Do you see what an additional joy it is for us when God chooses to answer prayer this way, by granting us to do miracles? This was the joy of the martyrs, who prayed to be obedient even unto death, who wished to witness to the greatness of God, and whose prayers were answered in their very persons! For their dying was like sunlight in a dark world. Their dying was miraculous even in the eyes of those who did not believe, for they died without narcotic; they died without some psychotic illusion; they died with their eyes wide open and yet died in a perfect peace.

The apostles, when they had been beaten, "left the presence of the council, rejoicing that they were counted worthy to suffer dishonor for the name" (Acts 5:41).

And Stephen, who had gazed into heaven and had seen Jesus standing at the right hand of God, is a biblical example of one whose prayer was answered by a holy dying, in whom the presence of the Lord Jesus was thus revealed. "As they were stoning Stephen, he prayed, 'Lord Jesus, receive my spirit.' And he knelt down and cried with a loud voice, 'Lord, do not hold this sin against them!' And when he had said this, he fell asleep" (Acts 7:59–60).

Thus the prayer of the martyrs and the beautiful answer of God even within them that prayed.

And though we may not have to die for the Lord, we may find, as they did, his word, his thrilling word, uttered within our persons and our performance, holier than we knew we were.

‿‿‿‿

"I slept in the same big bedroom as two of my brothers. My younger brothers, six years old and eight years old when I was twelve. Their bunk beds were by the wall. My little bed stood near the door."

I said, "Do you want more coffee?"

The woman was no longer smiling. She peered deeply into her empty cup. She shook her head.

I said, "Are you sure you want to tell me these things?"

Swiftly she touched the back of my hand. "It's okay, you know," she said.

But I felt a knot in my throat. I went for coffee and returned.

She said, "The first time my father came and lay with me he did not speak a word. For a while I thought that he was sick. I thought he was crying. But then he hurt me and I didn't understand.

"A chifforobe divided my bed from my brothers'. I think my father thought that we were hidden behind that chifforobe.

"He came back. He almost never talked. He apologized once, but he said, 'I am trying not to groan.' And once he said that this thing was just between us and I mustn't mention it to anyone else.

"Well, that's when I began to feel abandoned."

I sipped coffee. The woman had raised her eyes and was looking directly at me as she talked.

"Everyone in all the world respected my father. But what we were doing was so, so, so *wrong*. It was wrong in my heart and in my bones. I had long glossy hair in those days. My mother hummed when she brushed it. Beautiful sounds in her throat. Beautiful hair on my head. Long, long and beautiful. My father stroked my hair when he lay with me. It was my fault. My father stopped talking to me in the daylight. So did my mother. It was all my fault. So I crawled out of my hateful body. I went somewhere else when he was with me. I went somewhere else when I was with other children in school.

"When I was fourteen years old, I cut off all my hair. When she saw what I had done, my mother cried. But she didn't say anything. Whether my classmates were shocked or not, I didn't know. I didn't care. My father scolded me the next night that he came into my bed. So then I was wrong to have beautiful hair, and I was wrong to cut it off. So. I didn't care.

"Only this one thing did I do over and over, as if it were the Pilgrim's Jesus prayer. I prayed: *Love me, love me—Jesus come and help me. Amen.*"

She paused, as if hearing the prayer playing in her mind again, a soft refrain.

"Did Jesus come?" I asked. "Did he answer your prayer?"

"Oh, yes," she said, "and sooner than I knew."

By now it was three o'clock in the afternoon. The rain had stopped, but the day remained grey.

She said, "Would you get me some coffee now?"

I brought the pot and poured for both of us, then sat down.

"This is the sequence," my friend said, as if she were laying down a hand of cards. It must have been a hand she'd played often before. "In my sixteenth year my father stopped coming to my bed. I believe he had begun to fear that my brothers were not sleeping during his midnight visitations. But I don't pretend to understand my father's motives then. He just stopped.

"No one spoke of the secret after that, of course, and I remained estranged in the midst of my family.

"No one spoke of it, I say, until my youngest brother graduated from college. Shortly before he moved away for good, he took me out for a country drive. He pulled off the road into a little woods, then asked if I remembered our father's visits to our bedroom at night. I was stunned. I could only stare at him. There had never been words for this thing before—never!

"Well, he took my hand and started to cry and begged me to forgive him for never doing anything.

138

"He knew! My brother had known. How many others had known? Surely my mother knew! All at once the whole ocean of my grief poured out of me with a tremendous roaring. It was like to drown my brother!

"The fact that he was apologizing caused a switch to turn in my soul, filling me with a brilliant light and understanding: *No! It had not been my fault!* And I was furious. I hit him. He bowed his head and didn't fight back. I screamed and slapped my brother in his face. In a high, bloody jubilation, I cursed all of them, my father for hurting me so much and so long, my brothers just for knowing, my mother for her silence.

"'Why didn't you *do* anything?' I screamed.

"But all he said was, 'I'm sorry. I'm so sorry.'

"So I threw myself out of his car and walked away. My whole body was strong with anger. Anger felt so good in me.

"That was three years ago—the second event in the sequence. In the next months I confronted every member of my family and told them what they had done to me. I gave voice to the child they had wounded. I approached my father with a wild freedom. I mean, I didn't care what he did, whether he'd confess his sin, or deny it, or blame me. I didn't care, because my fury had set me free.

"But I wanted to crawl back into my own self again. Oh, I yearned for the consolations of peace. So I began to talk with a counselor, a calm Christian, a man clear regarding fault in the matter. It was not my fault. He repeated the message a hundred different ways, it was not my fault.

"But something kept troubling me.

"'I can't forgive them,' I told my counselor. 'I just can't. I mean, I am not able.'

139

"'I understand that,' he said.

"'But am I wrong *not* to? Am I still an evil person after all this if I don't? Do I *have* to forgive them?'

"And then that dear pastor preached for me a sermon I had never heard before. No, he said, I did not *have* to forgive them.

"He told me that forgiveness is of grace. It is a free gift, freely given, whose source is in the Lord. He said that an enforced forgiveness is not grace at all but a law which someone is demanding the victim to keep. Forgiveness which must be commanded is not forgiveness at all. Yes, they *needed* forgiveness, the pastor said; but let them go to its true source. Let them confess their sins unto the Lord Jesus Christ, whose forgiveness is their salvation. But I, he said, I did not *have* to do that which I *could* not do."

All at once the dining room brightened and my friend cast a shadow across our table. The sun had cracked the northwestern cloud. She turned and looked at it, then she turned back to me, smiling.

"Now I will tell you the truth," she said. "Jesus was there all along. I verily believe that it was Jesus who needled the soul of my younger brother until he confessed. And through that year of confrontations and counseling—the third event in my sequence—Jesus granted me first the anger of separation and independence, and second the peace of his grace.

Love me, love me—Jesus come and help me. Amen.

"He did. He answered my prayer.

"But it was not until the fourth event in my sequence," she smiled, "that I saw the full evidence of it.

"One morning last December, I woke up and discovered that I had forgiven my family. All of them. That's it." She smiled, spreading her fingers flat on the table.

140

"Maybe I forgave them in my sleep. I don't know. Only know that I woke up with true forgiveness in my heart.

"Or perhaps I should say that forgiveness was given me to give to them. You see? I was free of their sin. I was free of the pain it had caused me, free of hatreds and blame and keeping accounts. And here's the kicker, Walt: I loved them. My parents are no beauties. My poor parents scarcely know what a blessing I have for them whenever they're ready to receive it.

"It's right here," she said, touching her breast. "Blessing is right here, completely free and pure for them."

The woman suddenly grew sober. She did not remove her hand from her breast. She began to blink rapidly, for the thing she was about to say was so important.

"It is Jesus here," she said. "Here in me is Jesus, my dear Lord and the answer to my prayer. Because," she whispered, *"I could never have forgiven them their sin on my own.* It simply was not me. Even now it isn't me. It is Jesus who grants me my freedom with their forgiveness. It was Jesus all along.

"Walt, do you understand?" she said. "How Jesus answered my prayer was by causing me to do the thing that only he could do: miracles!" She giggled. "You are looking at a miracle-worker."

13

SPEAKING THROUGH THE
SCRIPTURES

*M*idway through his ministry, a lawyer (one who studied the laws of God) rose to ask Jesus a question. In fact, he asked the fundamental question: "Teacher, what shall I do to inherit eternal life?"

Thus did the man pray.

And the Lord listened.

Straightway, the Lord answered—and his answer directs us to another most significant means by which God regularly speaks to us: "What is written in the law, *Torah*? How do you read?"

As Jesus spoke, the man listened.

Then the man spoke again. He quoted two passages from the Books of Moses: "You shall love the Lord your God with all your heart, and with all your soul, and with all your strength, and with all your mind; and your neighbor as yourself."

Jesus listened.

And when the man had finished, he answered: "You have answered right; do this, and you will live."

When we read this brief exchange in Luke 10:25–28, we pay attention to its content, the laws of righteousness: love God, love your neighbor. Shortly Jesus will define "neighbor" by telling the parable of the Good Samaritan.

But the *form* of the exchange is also wonderfully instructive. It touches upon two significant principles regarding prayer, each so basic that it might be overlooked.

1. We have indicated often that prayer consists of four separate and distinct acts. But several of these acts may be repeated over and over in a single prayer. The prayer, then, may become an extended conversation between God and us. In that case it will consist of more than four parts after all, and may continue through time as God exchanges listening and speaking with us at a tender length. Watch what happens between Jesus and the lawyer.

Surely, one of the transported joys of our faithful praying is that it need not end at some fixed number of parts. If, with the lawyer, we choose to answer God's answer to us, and if God answers our answer, why, communication has become conversation, and prayer has become a *dialogue!* There are four acts to praying, indeed; but there is no limit to the number of parts.

"Amen" does not conclude communication! It was never intended to. We ourselves have turned that word into the closing of the door. "Amen" is meant to embrace all we have just said in our own certitude, our faith, our urgency, our agreement. Jesus uses it at the *front* of his most significant pronouncements. "Truly, truly, I say unto you" is in Greek, *"Amen, amen, I say unto you."*

But *Amen* itself is a Hebrew word, a derivation of the verb which means "to be firm, true, reliable; to trust in, to believe in." Luther once said that "amen" meant "Yea! Yea, it shall be so!" Add to the, "It shall be so *for me,*" because the word alone was used as an exclamation by which listeners join in an oath which someone else was

143

making—or a blessing, or a curse, or a public prayer, or a doxology. They were affirming their readiness to bear the consequences of this acknowledgment.

You see? *Amen* has been used for millennia even as it is used today, as lusty agreement in the midst of preaching, as a quiet and private approval—but it need not be a *stop* sign. Not an abrupt *The End* as at the end of a novel. Not a conclusion. For prayer may roll through its four acts round and round, ceaselessly, like the wheel.

2. Jesus directs the lawyer to that place where God's words are already recorded: *What is written? How do you read?* In that gesture, Jesus presumes an important distinction regarding the Holy Writings. Surely they are meant as general, timeless revelations to a whole people. They shaped Israel. They prepared for the appearing of the Messiah. And they were initiated by a gracious God. No one had to ask for them. They were God's utterance because God *choose* to speak to the people, to us, to the world. They are not necessarily a part of prayer.

But they may be!

That's the principle behind Jesus' words. The Holy Writings can also become the specific, timely, personal response of a listening Lord to a single praying person. God allows us—the creatures of his hands, but creatures of his breathing and his image—also to initiate the communication; and then his majestic pronouncements can become bits of intimate speech in our ears.

When you pray, then, after you have spoken, listen by reading.

Surely we will study the Scriptures. We will always receive them as the immutable declarations of God concerning things both true and spiritual in the universe. We will find them profitable for teaching, for reproof, for correction and for training in righteousness, that we may be of God, complete, equipped for every good work. They shall proclaim Jesus to us as to the nations. They shall be analyzed in sermons and books.

But all those activities are of the *We*. When you pray, be *you* for a while. Be one alone with the Lord. Read the Holy Writings with devout intent and a listening heart, not at all presuming that you can analyze the meanings of things, but rather waiting upon the Lord. *Listen* for the Lord's voice as he begins to speak the old words newly, near to you, personally in that moment and in that place and just to you. He may cause one biblical story to grow huge, to reach out and embrace you as if with his own arms. No matter how familiar it had been before, that story will suddenly be *your* story, naming the thing your prayer had hoped for, explaining the thing you had not understood, comforting you, exhorting you, calling to you, answering you—but in the voice of the Lord your God.

Or the Lord may use but a single passage as his voice to you, a prophecy of the Old Testament, a word of Jesus in the New, a phrase from one of the Epistles, which, when you read/hear it, may quietly fill your soul with convictions of his presence. And when the present Lord thus has spoken in your ear, you shall be changed.

There has always been such power in the Sacred Writings.

During a dark period of Judah's history, Hilkiah the high priest discovered the Book of the Law (the core of the Book of Deuteronomy) in the temple. He gave it to Shaphan, the secretary of King Josiah, and Shaphan read it aloud to the king. Here is the power of God's Sacred Scripture, the words themselves, to change the one who hears in them: "When the king heard the words of the book of the law, he rent his clothes. And the king commanded Hilkiah ... saying, 'Go, inquire of the LORD for me, and for the people, and for all Judah, concerning the words of this book that has been found; for great is the wrath of the LORD that is kindled against us, because our fathers have not obeyed the words of this book.'"

And so it happens that the dialogue continues: God's word is answered by Josiah's; Josiah's plea is answered again by God, speaking through the prophetess named Huldah, who lived in Jerusalem in the Second Quarter. God (revealing how much had happened to Josiah at the hearing of his Holy Writings) says: "Regarding the words which you have heard, because your heart was penitent, and you humbled yourself before the LORD, when you heard how I spoke against this place ... and you have rent your clothes and wept before me, *I also have heard you,* says the LORD. . . . You shall be gathered to your grave in peace."

There is prayer in its wholeness, all its parts—and Scripture was the voice of God.

Again, centuries later—after the exile of the Jews, after many had returned to their homeland again, but while there was little righteousness and less hope in their hearts—Ezra the scribe stood up before the people and read aloud the Book of the Law. Then "all the people wept when they heard the words of the law." The personalized voice of God moves hearts through stages to humility and righteousness again. Seeing their tears, "the Levites stilled all the people, saying, 'Be quiet, for this day is holy; do not be grieved'"(Nehemiah 8:1–12).

Even so does the Lord God breathe new life into his written Word, speaking it again, again—but with holy intimacy into your listening ear.

A young man came to the Lord by night. He fell on his face and said, "Teacher, how shall I spend my life? What shall I do with it?"

The Lord said, "No, but the greater question is, Who are you?"

The young man said, "I am myself."

The Lord said, "Then answer your question yourself."

The young man said, "Teacher, I don't know the answer. That's why I came to you. What shall I do with my life?"

The Lord said, "Who are you? Unto whom do you belong?"

"I told you," the young man said. "I am myself. I belong to no one."

The Lord said, "Then ask No One to answer your question."

The young man thought: "If I cannot answer the question myself, how would it help to ask no one?"

He thought and thought about the words of the Lord, feeling ever more lonely and confused.

Finally he said, "Teacher, you tell me: who am I? Unto whom should I belong? And what does that have to do with the rest of my life?"

Now the Lord looked upon the young man with love and said, "If you are a child of my Father, you will let his Spirit lead you the rest of your life."

"O Lord," the young man cried, "I want to be a child of God!"

"Then your guide must be the Spirit of God—not logic, not your own good sense, not the motives of the marketplace, nor all the pleasures or the goals of humankind, but the Holy Spirit only. Then all questions shall be answered: your identity, your love, and your future, forever."

Late in the autumn of 1973 I stood at a professional crossroads, unable to turn one way or the other.

For four years I had been teaching English at the University of Evansville. I had already earned my master's degree and was nearing completion of the Ph.D. I enjoyed teaching. A career had begun to drop root beneath me. Just as well, seeing that Thanne and I had three children and would soon adopt a fourth.

In fact, I was spending that autumn far from home, finishing the doctoral course requirements and preparing for my language exams, one in German, one in Latin. In those days Thanne's contribution to this career was remarkable, parenting three small children alone, spending a season and half a season housebound. How could I undercut such goodness by switching careers now? How could I jeopardize the stability of our family by turning from something certain to something uncertain and, likely, impoverishing?

Yet that was the alternative before me.

The pastor of our church in Evansville had been inviting me more and more to share his ministry. Before I left for school, I'd been teaching the adult Bible class, working with youth, administrating the educational program, spending Friday afternoons with the pastor in order to discuss the lessons upon which he planned to preach next Sunday.

"You should be in ministry," he said.

"I'm teaching," I said.

"No," he said. "You should be preaching."

"I like to teach."

"Right. Teach in the Church *and* preach."

"Why are you saying this now?" I asked. "You know I'm leaving for graduate school in the fall."

"Well," he said, "I think you should be going to the seminary."

Graduate school was in the east, Ohio. The seminary he meant was in the west, Missouri. Had the pastor seen some shine in my eye when we talked? I don't know. But late in August 1973, mere days before my departure east, he and the Church council together presented me with an official call: to assist the pastor, to finish my seminary training, to be rightly and properly ordained, and so to enter the preaching ministry of the Lord Jesus Christ.

That was the crossroad.

I did not immediately say No. I carried the call document with me to Ohio.

While I lived in a scholastic solitude, homesick, I thought and thought about this call. While I produced academic papers of publishable quality, while I labored at my languages, while I progressed with distinction and success down the bright road of higher education, I paused at odd moments and stared out the window and thought and thought about this call. *Was* it a call? Was it really a call from God?

But that road was utterly dark to me. I could not see the destination or the life it would require me and my family to live.

My brother-in-law once said, with no humor, with perfect sincerity, "God expects his pastor to be poor."

My father had been very poor, and poorer than I knew.

Ah, but you see?—my father was a pastor after all. And my grandfather had been a pastor. And my *great*-grandfather, who all his life had been the cleric of a single rural congregation, making visitations in a black buggy, one horse and one dog. Yes, yes, I paused and thought—and thought, *How could I do this to us now?*

And I prayed.

I spent the autumn praying for some direction in this issue, radical in every respect.

September turned into a burning October. And the bright candle of October then diminished into a grey November.

In order to refresh my knowledge of the Latin language, I was translating several New Testament books from Jerome's Vulgate Latin Bible into English. Four evenings a week I sat in the tiny library of the Catholic Newman Center, pouring over their copy of the Vulgate, writing out my translations in longhand. First, the Gospel According to Matthew; second, the Book of Acts. Third, Paul's Epistle to the Romans.

By the time I was translating the eighth chapter of Romans, the nights were cold and completely dark. The light in my little library was dim, the space beyond my books all lost in shadow, my soul most small and lonely.

I translated the twelfth verse, the thirteenth verse of the eighth chapter, both without much thought or attention, a slow pedestrian business—and then the fourteenth verse presented itself to me:

Quicumque enim spiritu Dei aguntur, ii sunt filii Dei.

I bent over it and began to turn the Latin words into English:

For whoever, I wrote upon white pages, *are led by the Spirit of God* . . . And I stopped. The verse engaged me. What *about* those who allow the Spirit of God to lead them? I wrote again, the clear and simple Latin answer: *they are sons of God.*

Ah, dear Jesus, that is what I wanted to be! I wanted to be a child of God!

And so what? Had I just been presented with the defining principle?

Yes!

God spoke to me in that tiny library, in darkness and a little light, by means of the words of his Holy Writing:

Yes: let my Spirit lead you, and you shall be my child.

And where else would the Spirit of God lead? What sort of work would the Spirit be pleased to find in me?

I tell you truly, ambivalence was wiped from my soul. In that moment I ceased limping between two opinions. I was a child of God!

Therefore I closed the enormous Latin Bible, walked through the cold night back to my room, sat down and wrote two letters: one to my Church saying that I accepted their offer; one to my wife saying that I loved her dearly—and that our lives were about to take a radical turn to the west.

14

SPEAKING THROUGH
THE LIVES OF THOSE
WE PRAY FOR

*S*hall we pray for the healing of those who are sick? Of course.

But what is the proper motive of such a prayer? Our love of the sick one? Our desire for her health? Yes, of course. It is such love that drives us to prayer in the first place.

Yet the fact that we direct our prayers to *God* indicates, properly, two other correlative motives: our love for God, and our faith in his strength and mercy. More than anything else, even more than our affections for the sick one (please note how crucial this is to proper praying in times of distress), the deepest desire behind our praying must be that the Lord be glorified by a manifestation of his sovereignty! If our prayer truly seeks God's honor, then whatever word he chooses to speak shall be right and a fulfillment of that prayer.

So, then: when our beloved is sick, his spoken answer may be her healing again. In her is the word of the Lord, for which we will rejoice and be grateful.

On the other hand, his answer may not be in her physical health but rather in her spiritual courage and sustenance—even, and especially, when she does not get well. Are you ready to abide a continued illness and to recognize God's sovereignty in a most *healthy* soul? Then you will hear a perfect and holy answer to your prayer.

Or the Lord may call that soul home. Again, (1) if your prayer was not motivated by self-serving desires but by the deep and faithful desire for the glory of the Lord, and (2) if you can "hear" the voice of God in his sovereign action, you shall recognize the answer of your prayer after all—since the Lord and your beloved will be well-met in heaven, without tears or sorrow or pain any more. The highest glory of God, the most wonderful gift he has for those whom we love, is their eternal life in his presence!

✺

Do you pray forgiveness for particular sins against particular people? I do. I become so painfully conscious of the pain I cause, whether purposeful or accidental, that it troubles my waking and my sleeping until it is made right again by God.

Especially in the household: because I love my wife and do dearly love my children, I grow mute with grief when I have somehow caused them to suffer. My prayers for forgiveness, then, beg life for a drowning man and peace for his family.

And surely, God hears the repentant heart. God answers by enacting an atonement. At-one-ment. It is the sweeter flow of Christ's blood from the cross.

Yes, he says in the third part of this prayer, *I forgive you.*

But the word of his answer shall be a cluster of deeds.

Yes is the renewal of our personal, childlike relationship with the Lord himself: *I love you.*

Yes, next, is the visible restoration of health to those whom we hurt, the genuine repair of the tender things we destroyed. The dear ones against whom we trespassed do survive and grow glad again: *I love them, too.*

Yes, finally, is the return of our beloved friends to our arms again, both healthy and unjudging. And these last two responses are evident even in the material world.

God answers. God speaks. And those who listen in the true humility of confession shall hear him clearly, for they will realize that the return of love is a divine gift. But those who do not confess will assume they deserve the love, and though God shall have said the same word to both, this latter group will hear no holy voice at all.

Oh, how often I have crept into the nighttime bedrooms of my children and watched them sleeping in milky innocence! But I've watched in sorrow, assailed by the memory of my angers, my harsh words, my overbearing demands. And I have sighed—I, who shouted for silence that afternoon because I was tired. I drove them to their rooms with tears in their eyes. *Fathers, do not provoke your children to anger, but bring them up in the discipline and instruction of the Lord* (Ephesians 6:4). Yes, yes, and the discipline of the Lord is to be patient and kind, not to insist on one's own way, not to be irritable or resentful, to bear all things, to believe all things, to hope all things, to endure all things (1 Corinthians 13:4–7).

Ah, what a miserable father I have been!

"Lord Jesus," I prayed in those dark nights, consumed by the vulnerability of such small people, "can you forgive me?"

And this was his spoken response: that the children came to me the next day completely new, with bright, clean eyes inquiring after my fatherly affection. And even today the Lord continues to answer my prayers in the present relationship our grown children have with us. Joseph and Matthew and Mary and Talitha—ages twenty-two through twenty-five—honor and love us. It is not our deserving; it is the forgiveness of the dear Lord made manifest in a dark world.

It is the extended communication between the Lord and me, a continuation of that same prayer, *Forgive me.* I have not forgotten what I uttered in such need; nor am I deaf to God's gracious answer. In the persisting love of our children doth he whisper over and over again, *Yes! Yes, yes, yes, yes, I have forgiven you!*

⁊ᛗᚢᎧ

So we pray blessings upon the heads of those whom we love, and the word of God occurs in their being blessed.

The reversal of this pattern may also be true: that someone who loves you may, without your knowledge, speak to God on your behalf—and God's response may be palpable changes in yourself. Not always does good fortune come of fortune merely. It comes of mighty conversations which mortals have with Immortality.

A few years ago I discovered that my father has been busily engaged in a daily prayer for the sake of the members of his household. Me included.

I was giving a public reading of my latest book in Colorado Springs. My parents attended the reading. During my preliminary remarks I asked them to stand, and before the audience I praised my father extravagantly. I described how his storytelling in my childhood had been the baby-beginning of my career as a writer.

After the reading was done, a long line formed—people seeking my signature in copies of my new book.

At the very end of the line stood my mother, her arms folded, her mouth closed.

When the line had diminished to its tail, when my mother alone was left, she said, "Wally, you should know that Dad prays every day for humility."

I said, "Ah, Mom, he deserves the praise. At his age it is surely time for me to speak public thanksgivings to him."

My mother stepped forward, grabbed me by both shoulders, stared deep into my eyes and said, "Humility for us *all*, Wally—for us *all*."

Ahhhh. For me, too. And, according to my mother's passions, for me especially.

In that moment I experienced bright flashes of recognition: certain events in my life were not at all haphazard. God had been in them—God and my father, muttering to one another about me, muttering, according to my mother's fierce pieties, about me especially.

For example:

I have always believed that my various professional roles are all in the service of the dear Lord, giving glory unto God.

Several years ago, while I was still pastor of Grace Church, one member of my congregation worked as a hot-line operator: Gloria Ferguson, a woman of killing sympathies. Even today she cannot abide the distress of any human, and she will not cease to pursue his ease until someone she trusts is as committed to it as she is.

One Saturday she telephoned me, anxious for a man "ninety-seven years old," she said. He'd called the police to report that he hadn't eaten in two days because that's how long his son had been missing.

"The cops gave me the case," Gloria said, "but I can't get a single agency to go out and help him. They're closed on weekends. I'd go, but I can't leave the phones. Pastor, will you go to him? Please? What if he died and we hadn't fed him?"

I went.

I, a pastor of some repute, put juice and soup and bread in a bag, and I went. I am an author. I am a lecturer, a voice within the global church, one sought for his counsel by leaders both secular and religious—a friend, in fact, to movie producers and television executives. Nevertheless, I drove to a ramshackle house, walked up to a torn screen door, rapped crisply (enjoying a certain greatness of soul)—and I went.

There was no answer, though the front door opened into darkness.

I rapped again.

"Well," screamed a voice within, "what are you waiting for?"

I pulled the screen door back and stepped inside. Before my eyes adjusted I smelled urine and heard soft popping sounds all around. Then I began to discern the man in his chair. Ninety-seven years old, a rangy skeleton, sockless, shoes untied, crumbs on a two days' growth of chin-whiskers, potato chips in his hand—he crouched in his chair, glaring at me.

The popping sounds were roaches dropping from the walls and hitting the wooden floor.

Since the old man said nothing, I said, "You are alone. You are hungry—" I reached into my bag and brought out a can of soup, but suddenly he hunched forward and screamed at the top of his lungs: "Kitty-kitty-kitty!"

There was a crash in the house's interior, then down the hall four cats came bounding at speeds of attack.

When they saw me, they stiffened their legs and slid to a stop, hair straight up. They glared at me, too. And the old man began to make a leaking sound, a paroxysm of soundless laughter.

"Ain' lonely, no," he cried out when he could. "Ain' lonely 'tall, no, nor hungry neither. Got my cats!"

"Well," I said—I hadn't sat; I was still standing— "then perhaps you don't need this soup—"

"Leave the soup!" he screamed. "Leave the soup. I'm gon' show you where. I gotta show you sumpin else too. I *got* to—"

But he didn't directly show me something else.

That is, he tried to, but he kept getting distracted.

The old death's-head man would lean far forward from his chair, preparing to stand up. But by the time his face was down between his knees, he seemed to forget about standing, and he stuck there, staring at the floor, suddenly discussing a new topic altogether.

"The first times I fell," he shouted, "I hurt m'self, you bet. But I learned to fall. Got to *learn* to fall! The last thirty-two times I'm fine."

Now he slowly rolled backward into the chair again and looked up at me. "No feelin' in the legs, you know. Here's the trick: don't wait for the fall. Got to rubber into it. What did ya say yer profession was?"

All this at the level of shriek. I'm an important person whom this skull is shrieking at. And I should be working on a sermon for tomorrow.

But he earnestly wants to show me something in the kitchen, so he leans forward again, but halfway forgets, quits and cries out: "Looky my arm!" Inches above the floor, he pinches himself. "Meat!" he shouts. "Good meat there! An' you know why?" He slumps backward and blinks. "On account of, I live right!"

158

"Sir," I say, "the kitchen?"

"What," he screams, "are you waiting for?"

This time when he leans forward and peers down between his knees, I put my hands under his armpits and lift him. I support him as we shuffle up the hall. Roaches flow from our feet. Cats curse our passage. The man is light, but his odor makes him seem awkward to me and heavy.

"Tomfool boy ran away," he bellows.

"What boy?" I ask.

"Missing person! Missing person!" he yells in my ear. "I'm gon' *shoot* him when I see him. Done run off once too many. Here! Stop! Here!"

We've come to the kitchen—and the kitchen is FULL of food!

The old man has covered a table and counters and an open ironing board with cans and bags and dried goods.

But "Here! Here!" he screams, pushing my small bag aside and pulling me toward a refrigerator.

"Here."

He opens the refrigerator door. Groggy roaches move among this larder too, all stuffed with food. Yet, here is his urgent desire, for the old man pokes among the packages and mumbles, "Butter. Bring butter. An' milk. An' some Philly cream cheese—"

A delivery boy!

I am a delivery boy for an old man who intends to pay me nothing, no, not so much as a compliment!

In the immediate moment I was furious— pastor/author/lecturer, reduced to a factotum!

But in the next moment, as if spontaneous fires had started in my heart and spread throughout my being, shame burned within me.

A *pastor,* am I? And my public roles are meant to serve God? But if I require honor and acknowledgment, and if I am insulted by the lack of these, then whose is the glory after all?

Isn't the most devout service to God that which receives no reward, not even the payment of praise, because then it is given completely unto the Lord? Yes: when I gain nothing, then my labor is my Lord's. And when I have become nothing, then I am myself the Lord's indeed.

It's a humiliation to be nothing. Therefore we seldom seek it. Yet, it must perforce return all glory to the Lord alone. Therefore, for one who loves the Lord, such humiliation is a goodness and a gift.

Thus, in a kitchen whose table groaned with food, insult turned into shame, and shame into humiliation, and humiliation into a glad humility after all.

That screaming, stinking, presumptive, ninety-seven-year-old man had blindly worked a change in me. No, I surely was not as articulate about that change then as I am now, but between now and then I have discovered what sort of mighty conversations were at the source of my change.

Dad prays humility for us all, Wally. For us ALL!

160

15

SPEAKING THROUGH THE CREATED WORLD

One Sabbath, years ago, when we were strolling home from church—through the neighborhood where my sons strove to maintain good reputations in the delicate society of adolescence—I mortified them by crying: "Look! That tree is your sister!"

I was feeling spasms of kinship in my bosom.

She was a radiant maple, burning in the autumn sunlight, her leaves green in their hearts but at their fringes fiery. I walked forward and stroked her magnificent trunk and explained: "She shares your breathing and the wind. She shares your thirst and the water. She shares light and life and sleeping and waking. She is your sister."

The boys grinned and dipped their heads—as if to nod, but actually to hide their faces from friends of more pragmatical attitudes.

That which I was then experiencing and espousing is considered "primitive" in the contemporary mechanistic culture—or hopelessly romantic.

"Dad, it's just a tree."

It's potential lumber. It is of an order fundamentally different from humankind. It is to be possessed and cut and nailed—reconstructed for bodily human benefit.

Ah, but if that's all we are able to make of nature, then we have deafened ourselves to one of the richest means by which the Lord God speaks to us!

Praise the LORD from the heavens [sings the Psalmist],
Praise him, all his angels,
  praise him, all his host!
Praise him, sun and moon,
  praise him, all you shining stars!

PSALM 148

⌔

More recently I entered a silent canoe alone and slipped from the shore to the surface of a northwood lake. Again, the earth was drawing an autumnal cover over itself.

I paddled the rim of the water. Sometimes the sunlight sank to the green bed underwater and laid my shadow there. Sometimes it hid behind the bordering forest—and then I paddled in the soundless shadows of the wood.

I found a narrow creek, a shallow current escaping the lake, and let it carry my canoe into a yellow meadow. Lily leaves and reeds brushed the hull like a passing hair, and I flowed unobstructed through a winding way. I saw crawfish shoot backward; I saw minnows dart through this living water.

Dragonflies attended me so nearly that we sat still in warm air, while the meadow moved backward, backward.

Soon I entered another, larger lake, and then it seemed that I was wholly alone in some primeval place among the silences.

A light wind got up and blew—and suddenly that shock of kinship seized my bosom again. No, I was not alone.

Praise the LORD from the earth,
*   you sea monsters and all deeps,*
fire and hail, snow and frost,
*   stormy wind fulfilling his command!*
Mountains and all hills,
*   fruit trees and all cedars!*
Beasts and all cattle,
*   creeping things and flying birds!*

The wind stirred texture on every living thing. The wide water ridged and rippled and softened under the dimple of my canoe. The lake was shivering exactly as my skin shivers. The leaves of the forest made a rushing sound, flipping and clapping in the millions around me. Here and there a tree released a stream of leaves like birds in long flocks, airborne. The whole forest was trembling exactly as my bones do tremble.

And I felt a profound familiarity. It was as though the skins which divide us from one another had melted, and the same singular force drove evenly through us all. All of us: the creek, the lakes, the forest, mountains and all hills, fruit trees and cedars and me. One force, one life, one wind exciting in us all the same glad reaction, the same dance, the same thanksgiving—the same choral praise for the Lord.

Let them praise the name of the LORD!
*   For he commanded and they were created.*
And he established them for ever and ever;
*   he fixed their bounds which cannot be passed.*

This deep sense of a natural kinship on a northwood water was for me an awakening unto peace.

It was a spoken word of the Creator who created all things first by speaking them. Unto me particularly, whose

163

life is so criminally hectic, whose prayer seeks healing and surcease, the Lord God said: *Shalom!* He said the word by means of creation, but then the word itself lodged in me, and what I became was the dear Lord's murmuring answer to my prayer.

Shalom: I was (at one with all that was) at peace. Restful, as on the original Sabbath, the seventh day of creation. Peaceful.

But how do I persuade my sons of this wonder, that creation vibrates both with praise *for* God and with the song *of* God in answer? How do I cause those who pray to rejoice in the union of all life in all its forms—since all, all is the handiwork of God, and all our praising is the same?

> *Praise the* LORD ...
> *Kings of the earth and all peoples,*
> *princes and all rulers of the earth!*
> *Young men and maidens together,*
> *old men and children!*

No, nature is not to be worshiped. And humanity is unique in the natural world, the emblem of the Deity, God's image here and the object of holy love. But if this sense of kinship is lost or benumbed in us or else scorned as a silly sentimentalizing of reality, then (1) creation is made vulnerable also to our unique sinning, and we shall (and we do) destroy without remorse the things God had placed in our care for the tilling and the keeping and the naming thereof.

And (2) we shall lose one of the richest, most tender, most endlessly various voices of the Lord God. The only "natural" word we'll be able to understand as divine shall be God's bellow of destructive power: storms, fire, earthquake, tornadoes. We will know nothing of still, small voices.

Desolating is that loss. For when he speaks through his creation, God can summon infinitely more expressions than human music and all our instruments. Indeed, the finest art we creatures can produce strives but to mimic the communications of the Creator: majesty and sweetness; sorrow, death and rebirth, the color green, the sound of a crawling worm inside the soil, the perfectly circular rainbow which can be seen only from free flight in tremendous heights.

The Lord himself makes connection between material nature and his more spiritual declarations. Listen how he uses creation as words to utter mercy:

> *For as the rain cometh down, and the snow from*
> *heaven,*
> *and returneth not thither, but watereth the earth,*
> *and maketh it bring forth and bud,*
> *that it may give seed to the sower,*
> *and bread to the eater:*
> *So shall my word be that goeth forth out of my mouth:*
> *it shall not return unto me void,*
> *but it shall accomplish that which I please,*
> *and it shall prosper in the thing whereto I sent it.*
>
> ISAIAH 55:10–11 (KJV)

Ask the farmer. Then sit down and listen through a long winter's night. For the faithful farmer has heard the word of the Lord in every season of the year, in every year of his life, in the soil and the sun, in water and wind and the freshening cow. And often the Lord repeats himself, for which the farmer annually rejoices (it is trust in the man and trustworthiness in God); but sometimes the Lord speaks words private and particular, for which the farmer is also prepared (his relation to God is personal after all, and not always easy).

Speaking of the Lord, who "fills you with the finest of the wheat," the psalmist contemplates the power of God's word, first to cause winter and then to become the spring:

> *He sends forth his command to the earth;*
> *his word runs swiftly.*
> *He gives snow like wool;*
> *he scatters hoarfrost like ashes.*
> *He casts forth his ice like morsels;*
> *who can stand before his cold?*
> *He sends forth his word, and melts them;*
> *he makes his wind blow, and the waters flow.*
>
> PSALM 147:14–18

O my sons, as you grow older, grow silent and still and as watchful as the farmer. For the word in a burning maple tree may be: *Shabbath.* Sabbath. Rest!

As trees do yearly withdraw, as the Lord on the seventh day rested, so you will need the peace in resting and the joy in praising God—or what good can all your other days hold for you?

16

GOD SPEAKS TO
ONE ALONE

*N**ight.**

*The dusk descends, and the streetlights string beads all
over the city, and the cars switch on their headlamps. People drive home. Their houses glow a while, but soon the doors
click locked, and the windows darken room by room, and
people go to bed. They sleep.*

*Midnight. A dog barks. Another dog joins the warning
with a long howl. But the alleys are empty. The two dogs woof
themselves back to silence and lie down and sleep.*

*Night. The small hours after midnight. All the world
is bedded now. All the world's asleep—*

෨෨

—But you, my child. You (says the dear Lord God):

You sit on your bed with your knees drawn up, gripping them with your arms. Why do you tremble? Why do you jump at the sound of two dogs barking? Why do you peer around at the walls and the windows?

"I'm afraid."

But this is your own familiar bedroom. What can you be afraid of?

"I'm afraid of the dark."

But the dark is no enemy—

"I'm blind in the dark! I'm lost. I can't see what's in front or what could attack me from behind or what I am or how protected I might be or *who* I might be—"

Faith, child!

Even in darkness it is my hand that leads you. I am here. My right hand holds you. For the dark is not dark to me, and the night is as bright as the day.

⁕

It is the night, and the whole world is sleeping—

—But you, my child, awake and alone. Why do you rise up? Why do you pace the floor so restlessly?

"For all that I didn't accomplish today."

But I saw you. You did a double day's labor.

"Not half enough! Time! Time! There is so little time and so much to do, and who will do it if I don't? I'm tired. I'm trapped. The night comes much too soon, and I can't keep working."

Rest, child!

Time is not yours to divide but mine to govern and by it to govern you. Who made the moon to mark the seasons? Who gave the sun its time for setting? Not you. I did that *for* you. The setting sun is a single deep command. I made the night so that the wide-eyed creatures might do their work. When the sun arises they will go obediently to bed; and then, in my good time, may you go forth to your work. But the night is dark so that dim-eyed fools are forced to sleep. Obey me. Let all labors finally be mine. Obey my celestial commands, and sleep.

⁕

"It's the night," you whimper.

I hear you, child. I see you cover your face and groan. Why do you heave such heavy sighs?

"When I close my eyes to sleep, the faces come back again. All the people I wounded today. My children, whom I cut with the edge of my tongue. My father, whom I cut with no word at all, by a resolute silence. My friend—

"Ah, one by one they pass me, frowning or weeping. And I am left alone. Even Jesus has abandoned me!"

Peace, child!

If you need signs in the night, look up. Can you count the stars that shine on you? Yet they people the velvet skies on your behalf. They are signs of my coming and our covenant together.

Look up. The stars that you see have ever been the hosts of heaven, serving me. I am the Lord of hosts; and these are angels. They are warriors when it is necessary to fight the evils that would consume you. But they have also all thrown "down their spears, and watered heaven with their tears": they are the choral angels who sang for shepherds watching over their flocks by night. They praise me and announced the birth of my Son.

Peace, they sang, for the Savior comes in spite of your sinning the day long. *Peace,* they sang, *to all with whom the Lord is pleased,* for by my Son do I come to forgive you, child, to enlighten and to love you.

Look up. It is a glorious, goodly company that surrounds your house and all the houses in the country, even the houses of those whom you hurt, but who are healing now precisely because they are sleeping in my night and in my care.

⚬➳

"Night! Night! Dear God, I am old and dying!"

Ah, my child, how you knot your sheets in terror.

"But the night feels like a grave, and sleep like a little death. Who's to say if I will wake again?"

Hope, child!

There is no sleep that does not have its waking. Do you believe that my Son died and rose again? Good. It is enough. For even so, through Jesus will I bring to myself all those who have fallen asleep. You need not grieve like those do who have no hope.

Death in the twilight? Death in the deep cessation of every night—is that what frightens you? Then let me comfort you with these words: every morning is a resurrection, and every sunrise bright with promise. For my Son will himself finally come to fill the sky with light, with a cry of command, and with the sound of the trumpet, and all who sleep the sleep of death will rise; and those who sleep in their bedrooms will also be caught up with them to meet my dear Son face-to-face. At the end there is no darkness at all—no, nor any real ending either!

Shall any night be hopeless then, if every sleep wakes up to such a light?

◊

"Oh, God! No one told me loneliness *hurts*—"

There was once a child who woke in a panic of loneliness. Immediately she screamed for her father. She howled with her head thrown back, like a wolf cub. She made such a roaring that she couldn't hear her father's whisper in her ear, assuring her that he held her life in his right hand, that he hung the moon in love for her, that all the stars were servants surrounding her, that he would be there to wake her in the morning.

Ah, it was not loneliness after all, but the *fear* of loneliness and all her moaning that isolated her.

Child, be still.

Be very still and listen. The night itself was made for the lonely, for my Spirit breathes best in darkness and in silences, and then my Word takes on most intimate and personal meanings. Everything that I have whispered in your ear tonight has already been written in my Book.

But when finally you can be still, then it doesn't matter how much the waters roar or how the mountains shake: in stillness you yourself will know that I am God, that I, the Lord of Hosts, am with you forever.

O my child, I love you. Rest in my refuge. Rest in my strength. Rest, and afterward—sleep.

FOUR

WE LISTEN

17

PREPARING TO LISTEN

n its simplest forms, the first act of praying happens naturally. As the infant cries out for its parents, so we, when in distress, cry to God. And though our prayers will develop over the years, growing in complexity, precision, obedience and wisdom, yet the basic act is born into us. It will happen.

The second and the third acts are God's. They, too, shall surely be accomplished: his omniscience listens, his love responds.

It is the fourth act—our own listening, our ability to be ever alert to the voice of the Lord—which requires a self-conscious preparation.

Surely, God can take us by our shoulders and shake us until we pay attention. But even that (amazingly!) doesn't always work (for the kingdom of Israel, in spite of prophets and signs and horrible shoulder-shakings, were scattered across the earth and vanished because they would not listen to the Lord). And when it does work, the shake may almost kill us (as it did the Jews who went into exile), as it did surely kill God's only Son on a cross.

Avoid such shoulder-shakings!

Allow the communion between yourself and the Lord to be as gentle as he wishes, as efficient and loving and personal, continual, comprehensive, rich, comforting, encouraging and true. Train yourself in the blessed practice of listening.

In the third part of this book, *God Speaks,* I touched often upon our listening. Just as we cannot separate our speaking from God's listening (he will, and his is the power that makes it work), neither can we separate his speaking from our listening (or we won't know that he has answered us). Morever, the different ways by which the Lord communicates with us require different kinds of awareness.

For that reason, you will recognize and remember some of the concepts offered in this chapter. In previous parts these concepts were associated with stories/experiences which gave them flesh. Here I will give them an orderly presentation so that you might see more completely the areas in which you may prepare yourself to hear the voice of God within the universe, and within your own ear, heart and soul.

18

PRACTICE THE PIETIES

The keenest ears unto the Lord are those freest of worldly concerns; quiet ears, ears unhectored by the clamor of self and pride; ears gladly alert to righteousness in others, sympathetically aware of sorrow; ears more and more familiar with the common voice of God.

Some listeners are born with these spiritual gifts. God has favored them, and we are blessed in their presence.

But most of us must learn the gifts of simple, humble, charitable living, out of which comes humble, generous and simple listening. We *learn* them because they bespeak a life antithetic to the life this world would have us lead: self-centered, more furiously complex, driven at speeds faster than the human heart.

Happily, Christians past have preserved for us certain private, pious disciplines that train us in behavior and lifestyle to hear the still, small voice of the Lord.

If our ears are not humble; if we already know what God should say to us (and therefore would be deaf to anything else God chooses to say); if all our conversation with God is filled with demand, turning the Creator into a servant and the created into taskmasters, then heaven itself will seem to us hatefully silent.

Therefore:

Give Alms

Give (as the old language states it) to the needy. I'm not advocating a mindless giving, as if your hand alone would push a dollar into the hand of a street beggar. Give with your whole being. Take time to choose the recipient of your charity (your *caritas,* your acts of evidential love). Know why the gift has been given (though you will certainly *not* try to control its use, or this will have been a gift with strings: givers who control are still imposing something of themselves upon the recipient and have not chosen true humility; pride remains).

It is not hard to recognize the needy. Jesus gives us a good list in Matthew 25:31–46. And Moses speaks eloquently of the righteous attitude with which one should give to the poor (Deuteronomy 15:7–11).

For this discipline to redound in blessing (training our ears to hear divinity) it cannot be a sometime, isolated act; it must become a way of life. As we watch *always* (kindly and creatively) for those who will benefit by our alms, so the focus of our deepest attentions will move out of ourselves and into the world—not into societies closed within their own self-sufficiencies and self-satisfactions, but into a world made open by need and hunger and disease and loneliness and poverty.

Note, please, that it is the act of charity that shall change and sustain you—not some calculable success on account of your act! Giving is *giving:* afterward, release it; it is gone. But the motive and the attitude of the act remain with you as a matter of genuine kinship with others and a personal gladness in yourself.

At the beginning of every year, Thanne and I pledge to our church a tithe (that is, ten percent) of our budgeted income for that year. But I'm a writer, and sometimes my income exceeds expectations. Thanne keeps an accurate record—and when November and December arrive, we are almsgivers of the ten percent that was not pledged before. So we watch! We must watch all year through for those most needy. College students in financial trouble; whole families failing; soup kitchens; individuals laboring in foreign countries; prisoners, or those who truly serve them; the sick. The need is as various as we have eyes to see them.

But I tell you of our practice only to assure you: what a humbling delight it is to serve God in this manner! We remain anonymous; but we experience a very intimate and personal relationship with the Lord by means of these recipients. I can hear God breathing in the night, as if we were runners side-by-side who achieve the same goal at the same time: friends.

And there is a further blessing in this practice: the face of God comes closer and closer to us, a daily presence all year through, the beautiful object of our watchfulness even in the torn human and the rejected!

෴

Several years ago my daughter accompanied me to New York on a business trip. Mary, inquisitive Mary, walked with me when my time was free. We traversed Manhattan.

It was March, raw and cold. Late in the afternoon we entered St. Patrick's Cathedral, partly for the warmth, partly for the glory.

The magnificent nave was filled with people, not just the tourist, the cleric and the devout but also the homeless, people whose lives were stuffed in plastic bags. Tourists kept moving, glancing briefly at anything curious or expensive. A good number of people prayed, sitting in the pews, kneeling, lighting so many candles in various side chapels that the hosts of heaven seemed present in flickering ranks to guard these small rooms of night. Some priests mumbled Mass at the altars protected by the mounted choirs of candles—holy gifts and memorials, no doubt, for people far away, but they seemed suddenly melancholy figures.

The homeless did not move much. They had staked out tiny territories, usually at the ends of pews, which they lined with old coats the way a bird lines her nest with string and down and paper. They sat. They dozed unshaven.

As we moved, Mary and I, up the left side of the nave, gazing at these chapels dedicated to saints, I took the opportunity to teach her.

"Nave," I said. "That's the main space in which people worship. The word comes from *navis,* Latin for 'ship.' Well, sometimes people thought of the church as a ship in which they sailed the perilous waters of this world to heaven. The anchor symbolized hope. Oh, and in Scandinavia they built their churches in the same design of their boats, but upside down."

Nave, I thought looking around and hearing the milling sound of a thousand secret voices, *it's a great ship filled with strangers now, and how many actually consider that they are only crossing the world-sea, that there is a shore on the farther side?*

My daughter said, "Yeah, but—" and fell into a brooding silence.

The saints in their chapels were shrouded in darkness. In the huge cathedral I felt the same as when I was a child in Grand Central Station, sourceless voices echoing from marble walls.

I pointed toward a saint whose eyes were rolled up toward heaven, a final cry before he died at the hands of unbelievers: Martyr.

"Martyr," I said to Mary. "People interpret that word to mean a holy death. They're right, of course. But in Greek it really means 'witness.' By their lives and by their deaths the martyrs *witnessed to* the presence and the power and the love of God. Like witnesses in a trail—except they were themselves the evidence."

"Yeah," Mary said, "yeah, but—"

My daughter is tall and blue-eyed and almost always content. *Born*—she cried when she was in high school: *Born to be a teenager!*

Now she twisted her lip in deeper contemplations. "But where's Jesus?" she said.

"Oh!" I said. "Well, up there where the side chapels end, near the high altar. Come."

The cathedral is cruciform; that is, with the transepts left and right of the altar, with the Lady Chapel on the far side of the altar from the nave, the building forms a cross.

Mary and I entered the space of the left transept. There on the walls were fourteen separate, life-sized sculptures of Jesus.

"They're called the Stations of the Cross," I explained. "They create a way of meditating on the love of God, because they tell a story with fourteen little chapters of Jesus' suffering and death and burial."

My long-legged daughter gazed at Jesus and Pontius Pilate, at Jesus shouldering his cross, at Jesus falling beneath its great weight, once, twice, three times.

"Well—" she said, "so there's a carving of Jesus."

She paused before each sculpture, still twisting her lip.

I glanced toward the high altar behind us. On the steps that mounted toward that holiest place—on the steps divided from the light and the beauty of the altar

181

by a metal grillwork—I noticed a woman bent severely in her spine. She was already short, covered in coats, but was so hunched that her head, hidden in babushkas, seemed lower than her shoulders. Like a crane's beak, there projected from her wrappings an enormous bulbous nose. Suddenly she turned in my direction, and I saw a heavy, heavy head sunk low upon this mushroom woman, a monstrous long head, great bags beneath her eyes, pendulous lips, and all as grey as ashes.

She looked to be the exaggeration of humanity, one of Disney's dwarfs or ancient teutonic sorrow, *Mother Holle*, a creature from under the earth. She descended the steps dragging a cloth bag behind her.

For Mary's sake I pointed to the thirteenth Station of the Cross, the body of the dead Lord Jesus as it is lowered from the cross.

"Sometimes," I said, "an artist will show Jesus dead in the arms of Mary, his mother. And then she is so sad. That scene is called *The Pietà*. It means 'the pity.' What do you think, Mary? Could anything grieve a mother more than to see the death of her child? The terrible, terrible pity."

My cheerful daughter grew solemn. "Dad, where's Jesus?" she said. Evidently her question had nothing to do with representations. Nor was she being childish. She was in those days departing adolescence. Her question bore tremendous weight after all, and more than I knew.

I blamed myself for teaching her gloom on a March afternoon in Manhattan.

"Come on," I said. "Let's stop at the Lady Chapel before we go out to find some supper."

The Lady Chapel is a space given unto itself. It surmounts the cruciform cathedral, a room dedicated to prayer alone, tranquil, hushed and beautiful. We stood at the entrance rail gazing at the backs of strangers as they knelt or sat in prayer. These were not at the moment tourists. They were supplicants. They were children of the Heavenly Father, worshiping.

I suppose Mary was counting her dollars against the meal we were going to buy. She was holding several bills in her hand when the long-headed, grey and weighty dwarf passed between us. The crouched woman paused and reached her right hand toward the holy water waiting at the gate.

In the instant before it touched the water, Mary took the woman's hand and put her dollars into it.

Old babushka turned her massive head toward my daughter and gazed up at her a moment. Mary, blushing furiously, curled her lips to smiling. The woman nodded as if she understood exactly what Mary had said, though Mary had said nothing at all—then she finished the reach for the water, crossed herself and crept up the aisle of the Lady Chapel, dragging her bag behind her. Just at the step where the chancel begins, she stopped. She stood still a long, long time; then slowly she went down the short space that separated her from the ground. She knelt, and I put my hand on Mary's shoulder to alert her to the holy thing. But she was the one who had given me sight. It was her spontaneous alms which taught me to see. The bent and heavy woman rose up again and turned and labored back in our direction without lifting her eyes.

"There," I whispered in Mary's ear. "Look there."

We watched as this ancient sailor moved past us into the nave again, this traveler down her own *via dolorosa,* this witness whose life *is* evidence, this least of the children of God.

"Never forget her, Mary," I said. "Never forget that you saw her face in the Lady Chapel in St. Patrick's Cathedral. Where is Jesus? There. In that woman."

⟨⟩

The alms-giving gives back, you see. Those who watch among the needy, seeking whom they may serve, will see in the needy the Lord himself—answering prayers in general and in specific and always in the very nearness of his presence.

Giving alms is no less than training ourselves to hear our God.

Fast

Not in public, not for glory, and certainly not to your body's detriment, but privately, for your soul's discipline.

If you choose to fast some particular kind of food or drink, something others take for granted, something whose absence, though it won't steal nutrition from you, will always be noticed by you, then this regular denial of your body's desire will continually turn you toward the Lord.

For it will remind you that you *are* created flesh, a creature bound in time between a birth and a death, whose physical needs shall not always be met. But awareness of your created state will alert you as well to the Creator, whose power you know in his creation, whose righteousness you know by the laws written in your hearts. And that cosmic awareness is but one step away from the arms of the Savior, who took upon himself a flesh exactly like yours, who also suffered denials—but for your sake! For love of you, and for your life hereafter.

When fasting has become a regular way of life, this sequence of spiritual awareness happens in a flash and persistently trains our grateful attention on Jesus, who speaks into the attentive spirit.

If you choose to make your fast a private matter (perhaps only your spouse or your best friend knows), then you will have to be alert in public, both to practice your fast and to keep it between you and the Lord alone. That will require an endless creativity, heading off questions and comments, but maintaining a full relationship with others. So you will be *busy* about fasting. Consequently, you will experience the irony of the Word Made Flesh, who was in the common world, busily ministering unto it, and yet who was "holy," separated from the common world for universal service.

Such a deep companionship between you and Jesus shall be like that between him and the disciples. You may grow to be the Beloved Disciple who lay on Jesus' bosom at the Last Supper, who stood at the foot of the cross and heard him murmur there.

Fasting for a specified period of time (a single day or a week under spiritual guidance) can have its own benefit, granting an intense awareness of the basic things in life, the body and the soul and the Creator and the Redeemer. And prayer under such a tight focus will also tune your ear to God's speaking. To those who have withdrawn from the hurly-burly life, the Lord will often speak directly by a palpable quietness in their spirits. Ah, such a wonderful peace!

Pray

Understand that praying is its *own* piety, that the doing of a thing empowers you to do it better and better.

Regularize prayer for yourself.

Pray in private, in the same place, at the same time every day. Give the act your full, deliberate consideration, doing nothing else but praying. Contemplate the things of God. "Contemplate" derives from *temple,* being in that place where the sacred is made evident. Pray: seek the sacred to ponder it.

You may repeat the same prayer over day after day. I recommend it. No, don't pray the sound only, but concentrate all your spiritual attention upon that prayer each time you pray it. Live in its large rooms a while, then in time find its subtleties, its small corners, its deeper faith and insight.

There is enormous blessing in this repetition—especially for people who tend mostly to pray the spontaneous prayers of their hearts. After a period of time, spontaneous prayers do in fact begin to resemble each other and therefore become a shallow means of communicating with God. But if you choose the prayer of another (the Lord's Prayer; Solomon's prayer at the dedication of the temple; a particular psalm; St. Francis of Assissi's "Canticle of the Sun") and if you pray that prayer day after day for an extended period of time, the prayer eventually will speak to you and then *for* you. Praying the prayers of the faithful will train your whole self, heart and mind and ears, to hear as the faithful heard.

Such a regular discipline of prayer, then, is the shaping of your spirit; it becomes for you a way of life; it is, therefore, its own preparation for hearing the voice of God. This is the practice of the "elect," those who live in covenant with God, just as my morning greeting to Thanne is a practice of my covenant with her. We give each other the same greeting, day after day; but the day would lack shape without it.

Read the Lord's parable in Luke 18:1–8, which he told to the effect that people ought always to pray and not lose heart.

Let me now elaborate on the details of your regular prayer time: you may make a sort of "sandwich" of it. Both begin and end with the same two prayers every day to accomplish what I've noted above, but then fill the time between with prayers for particular people in your community, in the sphere of your knowledge. You need not tell them that you are praying for them; but as you do your heart cannot help but turn godly toward them. Now the private discipline becomes communal, and you submerge yourself in the need of others and the power of God. You diminish.

This is the humbleness that shall surely hear the voice of God and hears it without shock or surprise; for to pray for others is to strengthen that faith which *expects* God to respond in love.

Worship

—regularly within your committed community of faith. Whatever else shall happen in worship (much of which you yourself may add here) this most necessary transaction takes place: the body of believers expresses in many ways the Godship of God, and the glad, obedient submission of his faithful people.

"Worship" comes from the Old English word: *weorth-scipe*. It might be translated "worth-ship." *Scipe* indicates a state or condition, like king-*ship*, steward-*ship*, friend-*ship*. But here it refers to the deep condition of God: that all *weorth*—all worthiness, value, repute, reverence, respect—belongs only unto God.

So the gathered body of believers not only declares God worthy; not only offers all worth to him in hymns and anthems, in gesture and litanies and preaching and prayer; but it also actually renews that right relationship

187

between itself and its God. This is more than a memorial, a remembrance of things past; this is an actual event; something happens! And you, when the living body of Christians around you turn faces brightly toward the Lord, are by their communal action turned as well!

Now you are more acutely attuned to the voice of the Lord God. And since God "inhabits the praises" of his people Israel, he makes an immediate and direct response: during worship, he speaks *through* the multitude, through the selfsame expressions by which they pray!—in their hymns, their various praises; in the devout pressure of their collected bodies and souls; in the Scriptures read, in sermons, and in personal witnesses. Worship, then, is the formal closing of the circle of divine conversation. It is prayer made whole even in *that* time and in *that* place, the perfect piety for the weak, the immature, the person who feels too crippled to pray well, or to pray at all. In worship, hear the prayer *and* hear the Lord's answer, week after week after week, until you know the song and the tune on your own.

Then go home and sing in your solo voice the praise upon which God himself will sit enthroned.

19

ASSESS, CONFESS, GET OUT OF THE WAY

t is so important that we know *ourselves* in order to listen to our Father with a discrimination and clarity.

Discrimination: to distinguish between God's true response and our loud desirings, which sometimes drown out God's voice. Noisy with anger, we may be deaf to mercy. Noisy with need, we may reject any word of the Lord which discusses topics different from those we thought were most important.

The self-centered supplicant is a dreadful contradiction. There are no other voices he can recognize, for he has made a god of *himself,* which is the original of all sinning. It is the sin that severed us from sweet Eden, cherubims blocking the east gate, and a flaming sword turned every way.

Again, discrimination: to recognize when we have *imputed* divine intent or agency to certain experiences which may be mundane first to last. Well, we do sentimentalize our religion, you know. We're inclined to see God and goodness in anything that moves us to tears. That's why *our* cherubim are chubby little children. Where we think we hear God we may be hearing our own emotions.

On the other hand, we do terrorize ourselves by religion and are inclined to see the hand of a wrathful God in accidents, injuries, deaths and sundry difficulties.

Now, the word of God may surely be in any experience. His word, as we have said, is deed, and his deed is our experience—yes. But human emotion is never the best interpreter of that word. The Bible is the final and true dictionary by which we can accurately interpret God's speaking unto us. The Bible reveals the meanings of the acts of God. It is by a genuine and faithful study of Scriptures that we can recognize the hand of a merciful God, a saving God, a punishing God, a God of a thousand topics.

So you think that a moment of ineffable joy was divine communication to you. How can you be sure?

1. Find another such moment of similar detail and shape and purpose in the Bible; *there* is the word for which you need a definition; what does the Bible say about its moment? What does the whole context of the narrative have to do with that moment? How does it relate to the Creator? The Redeemer? The Holy Spirit? All these things will provide you with a definition for the experience in your life, and by these holy, recorded words of God will you be able to understand the word enacted for you.

2. Be sure that your interpretation of the event which happened to you does not contradict the teachings *or* the narrative in the whole of the Bible, Genesis through Revelation. How important it is to have studied God's dictionary in order to discriminate with clarity the words of God uttered in your own life.

⌒〰〰〇

Study of the Holy Bible, then, is necessary preparation to hear well the voice of God. It is the training of the mind.

But to hear the voice at all requires preparation of the soul, a training which must be more than teaching and learning. Since the soul is the inner ear by which we hear the Spirit in intimate conversation, we must regularly clean it out, purge it of sin and of the self that deafens it.

As long as David continued in sin, unwilling even to admit that his adultery was a sin, he could not distinguish the voice of the Lord from the voices of his own desires. But when he in sincere sorrow confessed his sin, *Wash me thoroughly from my iniquity, and cleanse me from my sin,* God said in effect, *Ephphatha,* and his ears were opened and he could hear the Lord again: *Cast me not away from thy presence, and take not thy holy Spirit from me.*

All this is a paradigm for us.

Unless we seek to know our sins and then to confess them unto God as the sins that have divided us by a flaming sword, the heavens will seem vastly silent to us, and all the world a lonely place—not because God is not talking, but rather because we cannot hear his voice.

⌇

Yes, and I confess my arrogance. In the desperate hunger to hear the voice of my Father, I confess the ministerial pride that closed me in a cave of my self.

I chose for several days to keep the curtain drawn between me and the man in my hospital room so that I could without interruption attend to my own affairs.

He lacked a leg, my roommate. He was paralyzed in his right side. Therefore, my will prevailed since he couldn't rise to reach the curtain, could not so much as turn himself in bed without assistance. Besides, he seemed so obsequiously concerned to please me in every particular, that he would never open what I had closed.

I hardly knew the man. He knew me not at all. I wanted to keep it that way. I wanted nothing from him but his silence and my privacy.

Well, consider my station: all week long, all my professional life long, I counseled people with troubles lesser or greater than his. I served the members of my congregation in jails, in their homes, on the street, in hospitals when I came but to visit. Now that I was myself the patient I deserved rest. That's a good reason to be left alone, isn't it?

And consider: I was facing major surgery. The questions that worried me then were elemental, and I was made uncomfortable by the terms of the barter, life and death. Good reason—wouldn't you say?—to be consumed with oneself alone.

Consider: I hadn't had a chance to read Shakespeare undisturbed since college.

Thereby did Walt excuse Walt for thinking of Walt alone and ignoring the man on the far side of the curtain.

But the man spoke in spite of all, to nurses when they came ministering, to the air, perhaps, when no one else was in the room.

"People are so good to me," he repeated over and over. "For nine years now so good and kind to me."

Well, then he was content with his life. No need for me to offer him anything else.

He praised the nurse extravagantly. I could hear the little sob-chokings in his words while she was turning him, "Thank you, thank you, thank you—" And then when she had gone: "These are such beautiful nurses here, don't you think?"

Me, I grunted.

When he used the bedpan, he did so with a persistent soft apology. "Sure does make noise, doesn't it?"

I grunted.

While he was waiting for the nurse: "Sure does make a stink, doesn't it?"

I grunted.

"Sure does," he said tremulously while the nurse was washing him, "make a mess."

All this he said in simple conversational manner. Yes, a man adjusted to his limited life. Never a bathroom. Never a toilet. Never in nine years a bowel movement without someone to help him.

Ah, but he repeated these same phrases day after day, every time his bowels moved, "Sure does make a mess," and then again, "Such beautiful, beautiful nurses we got here."

And, through the curtain, I grunted, shortening the grunt to brief barks of inattention.

"Yes," he said one evening, "nine years ago I was laughing like anybody. Eating a sandwich on the job. Telling jokes. Laughing, laughing, you know, like anybody. Then I leaned back, and bingo! Right there at lunch. A stroke. . . .

"But God's been so good to me since. Kept me alive in one operation after the other, when I should have died, should, you know, have died.

"Worked puzzles, you know," he said through the curtain.

And he said, "I'm a Bible scholar, too, like you. Read it every day."

I was all done grunting. He was creeping rather close to my personal self.

He said, "Does talking bother you?"

"Well," I said, clearing my throat, "I'm working on a few things here."

He said, "Oh, I'm sorry! I'm so sorry. I don't never mean to be a burden. Just say the word. I'm sorry, sorry—." And he fell silent.

How sorry he really felt I learned later that night. He rang for the nurse. In fact, he had to press his bedside button several times.

When the intercom crackled, "Can I help you?" he whispered very quietly: "Can someone please bring me my Bible?"

But I saw the Bible on the small table between us, just out of his reach, certainly within mine.

The next morning my doctor came to tell me that he was scheduling surgery for me after all. Two weeks hence. A thoracotomy. The removal of a portion of my right lung. There were distinct shadows. But I could go home as soon as he signed release forms. He shook my hand and left. I telephoned Thanne.

Within the hour I was dressed and pacing, brooding over life and death, waiting to go home.

My roommate broke the silence.

"Please? Please?" he whispered. "Please?"

I stepped around the curtain.

He was stretching his left hand toward me. "You're leaving," he whispered. "Please . . . ?"

And when I took his hand to shake it, remarkably, he burst into tears. He trembled and sobbed and nearly broke my bones with squeezing them.

"Wherever you go," he wept, "you have a friend in me."

Then he clung to me, and what the curtain had hidden for the last week flooded my seeing and my knowing.

Ah, what anguish hides behind stiff smiles and platitudes! And how many people encourage the suffering ones to keep their hard lives hidden! What loneliness we impose on one another!

No, no, of course my roommate was not content with his lot. He was agonized by nine years' helplessness, nine years' dependence upon others for the most common and private processes, nine years' indignity. He was weeping for one more loss. He wept to lose one who had given him just nothing at all. And he called that one a friend. How few friends he must have had, then, and how deep his sense of personal shame.

Have mercy on me, O God, according to your steadfast love! According to your abundant mercy, blot out my transgressions. For I am the cause of this man's loneliness. By my self-absorption and my grunting I shamed him one week longer in his life.

And this is the corollary to that sin: for one week I was deaf to the voice of Jesus in my hospital room. Since I sought service for myself, I ignored the least of his brethren and in consequence did not hear the Lord himself calling: *I am sick. Come, visit me.*

And now at my leaving it became apparent that in serving, I would have been served: "Wherever you go, you have a friend in me."

Well, yes! Our circumstances are not all that different, are they? I was just reading Shakespeare, talking, laughing like anybody else, and Bingo! They came to cut a part of my breathing out of me—

⁓

In order to make your confession regularly and with a thoughtful, scrutinizing self-examination, I suggest that you involve other Christians who will keep your confidence absolute, who believe in forgiveness, and who love the Lord Jesus. Confess to the Lord in their hearing. Allow them gently to question you until you have truly disclosed the whole of your sinning. And when all has been confessed out loud, then hear in the mouths of your friends the clear and certain assurance of Jesus' forgiveness.

I meet weekly with a colleague of mine here at the university. We speak of many things, but we do not part without having prayed together. We are steel sharpening steel when we pray, each God's gift to the other. In very personal terms we bring up our secret faults and utter them out of our souls, into the air, into the conversation of our faithful friendship. Again, in personal terms we each declare God's forgiveness for the other. And then we pray.

For several years while Thanne and I still lived in Evansville, we met weekly with a prayer group of eight people. To pray regularly with seven friends prepared each of us to hear the voice of the Lord for the rest of the week, when we were apart from one another. And when we gathered again, we would swap stories of how God had spoken in our lives that week. With every story one of us was a witness; with every story the rest of us were disciples, learning how to pray whole prayer in all four of its parts, learning the thousands of voices of the Spirit, learning how to listen.

In a group of eight, all of whom love the Lord, everyone may also *be* loved while no single person is allowed to dominate or else to demand love. We may esteem each other so kindly and so well, that no one need be lost in that desperate house of mirrors called "self-esteem." On the other hand, we may hold each other to standards of holy goodness and faithfulness. Each one, then, is helped by everyone to get his or her *self* out of the way of the Lord.

20

HUMILITY AND
THE SOUL'S SILENCE

*I*n the earliest days of the Christian Church, who had ears to hear the call of the Gospel? Why, those whose ears were empty.

Again, who recognized the voice of the Lord quickest, with easiest speed releasing their worldly associations for a lifetime with the Spirit of Christ? Those whose hands and whose souls were empty.

The hungry child is alert to the whispers of its mother. The full child, preoccupied with pleasures, neglects her strong voice and her pleas.

"For consider your call," writes Paul to the Corinthians,

> *not many of you were wise according to worldly standards, not many were powerful, not many were of noble birth; but God chose what is foolish in the world to shame the wise, God chose what is weak in the world to shame the strong, God chose what is low and despised in the world, even things that are not, to bring to nothing things that are, so that no human being might boast in the presence of God.* (1 Corinthians 1:26–29)

The early Church had a high population of slaves and women and people impoverished. They had the ears to hear.

It is the same among religious people of many religions: when one wishes to hear God speak, he empties himself, divests himself of goods, removes himself from clamorous society. The Lakota Indian goes out alone without companion, without food, without clothing, but with a deep sense of his smallness before God. Unhoused, naked, fasting, he cries under heaven for a communication from God.

And this is what he says: *Wachin ksapa yo!* "Be attentive when one no longer remembers himself, when his whole being is attentive to the earth and the sky and the spirit of God in them, he will hear God's message. Even the tread of an ant will sound as loud as thunder at his ear, and the sound will hold meaning."

What some may do for a while—in a timed retreat, on a vision quest—others do for a lifetime. These, committing themselves to greater service and greater simplicity, become for us saints and models of holy living. They bear witness to the practical reality, that *humility hears the Lord*. The less of self—the less of the self's attachment to this world, the less the self is defined by the status or the things of this material world—the more open is the soul to God's presence and God's ten thousand communications unto his beloved.

Thus the Friars Minor, the Little Brothers who took vows of poverty and humility as a way of life.

Thus Saint Francis of Assisi, who founded the Order at the beginning of the thirteenth century. "My brothers are called Minors for this reason," he once said, "that they should not presume to become greater. For their vocation teaches them to remain lowly, and to imitate the footsteps of the humility of Christ, that hereby at last they may be exalted more than others in the sight of the saints."

Once when a poor woman came to his place, Porziuncola, "the little portion," Francis looked round for something to give her that she could sell for bread. He could find nothing but the single copy of the Gospels which the friars possessed. So he gave her that.

Here is a story to illustrate both Francis' commitment to humility in worldly matters and his affection for those around him. An early friar, Brother Ruffino, came from a family of wealth and reputation in Assisi; but he himself was retiring, neither bold nor eloquent. Francis decided to strengthen the fellow in his practices and sent him into Assisi to preach in one of the churches there, wearing only his breeches, nothing more.

Well, the townsfolk gathered in the streets and mocked the poor, naked young man.

At the same time, Francis began to feel sorry for Ruffino and guilty for his decision; so he took off his habit and set off for Assisi himself in nothing but a breechcloth. He, too, was mocked. People howled with laughter. But he joined Ruffino in the pulpit and, as it is written, "preached so marvellously of the contempt of the world, of holy penitence, of voluntary poverty, and of the desire for the kingdom of heaven, and of the nakedness and shame of the passion of our Lord Jesus Christ, that all they that heard the preaching began to weep most bitterly with devout and contrite hearts."

And what did such humility grant Francis but in joy to recognize constantly the communication of his Lord, yes, even in this world.

In the *Speculum Perfectionis,* the "Mirror of Perfection," it is written of Francis that as he traveled with his companions about the countryside, preaching, "The most sweet melody of spirit boiled up within him frequently breaking out in French speech—and the veins of murmuring which he heard secretly with his ears, broke forth into French-like rejoicing."

There is truth to the tales that Francis lived in communication with the creatures and the creation of God. Of course: he recognized that he was a creature too, and his humility opened him to *every* utterance of the Lord God, even those that flew in the wind—the birds. Once when great flocks of birds enclosed him, he admonished them to praise their Creator, "for he has given you a dwelling in the purity of the air."

He tamed a ravening wolf.

He could command falcons to hold their peace till he was done with praying.

Francis set no great store by this ability. For him it was a natural, incidental part of a life intimate with God and the things of God.

Daily this man of most common, rough-hewn living rejoiced in the holiness of common things. During his last days, wracked with physical suffering, he began to sing a song of glory in the ordinary, the Creator in his creation. He sang the song that delighted in relationship, for humility made him brother to every created thing, every thing of which was a word of God. He sang the song of one who has learned to hear the Lord, to hear without ceasing. All four acts of prayer and bounden in this one:

> *Most High, Omnipotent, God Lord,*
> *Thine be the praise, the glory, the honour and all*
> *benediction.*

200

To Thee alone, Most High, they are due, and no man
is worthy to mention Thee.

Be Thou praised, my Lord, with all Thy creatures,
above all Brother Sun,
who gives the day and lightens us therewith.
And he is beautiful and radiant with great splendor,
of Thee, Most High, he bears similitude.

Be Thou praised, my Lord, of Sister Moon and the
stars,
in the heaven hast Thou formed them clear and
precious and comely.
Be Thou praised, my Lord, of Brother Wind,
and of the air, and the cloud, and of fair and all
weather,
by which Thou givest to Thy creatures sustenance.

Be Thou praised, my Lord, of Sister Water,
which is much useful and humble and precious
and pure.

Be Thou praised, my Lord, of Brother Fire,
by which Thou hast lightened the night,
and he is beautiful and joyful and robust and
strong.

Be Thou praised, my Lord, of our Sister Mother Earth,
which sustains and hath us in rule,
and produces divers fruits with colored flowers
and herbs.

In the year 1226, blind, growing weaker for certain
hemorrhages, he asked his physician, Buongiovanni, how
long he, Francis, had to live. The doctor hesitated, then
said that death was near.

"Welcome, Sister Death," cried Francis. Even in this event his pure ear heard the presence of his Lord, and he added yet two more verses to his song:

Be Thou praised, my Lord, of our Sister Bodily Death,
from whom no man living may escape.
Woe to those who die in mortal sin.

Blessed are they who are found in Thy most holy will
for the second death shall not work them ill.
Praise ye and bless my Lord, and give Him thanks,
and serve Him with great humility.

But finally we must turn to the supreme model of One who knew how to hear the voice of God.

When Jesus prayed, he prepared for his Father's answer in ways which every Christian might imitate. Especially when there was a specific topic of conversation on his mind, he withdrew into humility and the silences.

Watch:

"In these days he went out into the hills to pray; and all night he continued in prayer to God."

The method is both physical and spiritual, an external as well as an internal alertness. And here he has something of cosmic importance to discuss with his Father, therefore his preparation is one of genuine solitude.

What topic?

"When it was day, he called his disciples, and chose from them twelve, whom he named apostles" (Luke 6:12–13). The topic regarded the root and flower of the Church on earth. Of course Jesus prayed in a place utterly alone, apart from the distractions of the world, cleansed of any interest save his Father's wish, his Father's voice.

So he chose "Simon, whom he named Peter, and Andrew his brother, and James and John, and . . ."

Throughout the Gospels there are countless instances of lesser withdrawal, the same type of preparation over and over again. Why, his entire life exhibits the humility that hears the Father: for Jesus, "though he was in the form of God, did not count equality with God a thing to be grasped, but emptied himself" (Philippians 2:6–7). Even his daily life was one of a wanderer, more humble than that of the wild beasts. "Foxes have holes, and birds of the air have nests; but the Son of man has nowhere to lay his head" (Matthew 8:20). Jesus is the model. Francis was the imitator. So ought we to be—and the voice of God will arise for us, too, in common things and ordinary events.

But finally we find in Christ the most extraordinary example of perfect listening. The day before he died, at the very center of human history, Jesus became for us the paragon of prayer, for in his final praying all our prayer begins. His is the pattern for ours, he is the power, and his prayer declares the purpose of prayer in general.

Lord, teach us to pray!

And his answer finally would be more than "say": *When you pray, say* . . . For this will involve also one's *doing* and, more than that, one's *being*.

If you wish, read Matthew 26:36–46, and then watch:

Humility and obedience, divestment, solitude and the silences are profoundly evident in the most dramatic prayer Christ prayed on behalf of the entire world. Surely, this time he must hear God. And he must with drop-dead accuracy distinguish the voice and will of the Father from his own desires and his own emotions. Therefore, he who emptied himself of the powers of deity now must empty himself of the will and the wish of humanity.

This is the preparation of love—loving hungry humankind, too full of itself to pray properly, for its sin is that it will not hear the will of the Father.

This is the preparation of existential obedience—for the hearing that Christ is prepared to do now is *of body and soul,* not just of the ear and the mind. What he hears from God shall become the immediate activity of his life and death. His hearing shall be his next doing. That is the highest hearing, the most complete accomplishment of the fourth act of prayer. It is called obedience.

And so pure is Christ's preparation, so acute is his hearing, that he recognizes the answer of his Father in no word at all, no sentence, no act, no *thing:* but in heaven's perfect silence. Ah, *silentium tremendum!*

Jesus' ability to hear his Father outstrips even Elijah on the Holy Mountain, who learned to hear the Lord God in the "still, small voice," which is best translated: "a sound of gentle stillness," an eerie stillness so still that it can be heard. Elijah's silence of God surrounded a mountain.

But the silence that Jesus endures and understands is for him *divine absentia,* the absence of God through all the halls of the universe.

Again, then, watch:

> Then Jesus went with them to a place called Gethsemane, and he said to his disciples, *"Sit here, while I go yonder and pray."*
>
> And taking with him Peter and the two sons of Zebedee, he began to be sorrowful and troubled. Then he said to them, *"My soul is very sorrowful, even unto death; remain here and watch with me."*

And going a little farther he fell on this face and prayed, *"My Father, if it be possible, let this cup pass from me; nevertheless, not as I will, but as thou wilt."*

And he came to the disciples and found them sleeping; and he said to Peter, *"So, could you not watch with me one hour? Watch and pray that you may not enter into temptation; the spirit indeed is willing, but the flesh is weak."*

Again, for the second time, he went away and prayed, *"My Father, if this cannot pass unless I drink it, thy will be done."*

And again he came and found them sleeping, for their eyes were heavy. So, leaving them again, he went away and prayed for the third time, saying the same words.

Then he came to the disciples and said to them, *"Are you still sleeping and taking your rest? Behold, the hour is at hand, and the Son of man is betrayed into the hands of sinners. Rise, let us be going; see, my betrayer is at hand."*

Imitate Christ!

Recognize how much love must be motive and preparation for your highest praying, love for those whom God has placed into your care; recognize how much love of others is a surrender of personal wish and will, a genuine opening of your soul's ear to hear the Lord. This is the second most important preparation.

And the first most important preparation is this: that you love the Lord your God with all your heart and with all your soul *and* with all your mind. This love is the complete emptying of self. It listens with heart, soul *and* mind. And its listening is manifest not just in knowing—that you have heard some information from God and now you know more than you did. No, its listening is manifest also in *doing*, how you act, how you behave, for such listening is obedience. And finally listening in the love of God is manifest in *being*, who you are and what you are becoming the more and more the voice of God is your thought, your heartbeat and all your self.

Whole prayer grows into the wholeness of divine relationship.

O my God, when will silence, retirement, and prayer become the occupations of my soul as they are now frequently the objects of my desires? How am I wearied with saying so much and yet doing so little for you! Come, Jesus, come, you the only object of my love, the center and supreme happiness of my soul! Come, and impress my mind with such a lively conviction of thy presence that all within me may yield to its influence. Amen.

THOMAS À KEMPIS

Walter Wangerin, Jr.
September 25, 1996

Other Books in the Growing Deeper Series You Will Enjoy

Church: Why Bother? My Personal Pilgrimage by Philip Yancey

Disarming the Darkness: A Guide to Spiritual Warfare by Calvin Miller

Water My Soul: Cultivating the Interior Life by Luci Shaw

The Wisdom of Each Other: A Conversation Between Spiritual Friends by Eugene H. Peterson